ELEVATING TRUST IN LOCAL GOVERNMENT

*The Power of Community-Based
Strategic Planning*

RICK DAVIS & DAN GRIFFITHS

ISBN: 978-1-944141-37-0

Printed in the United States of America

Book design by Morgan Crockett

Cover design by Mikaela Smith

Dedicated to the thousands of volunteers
who selflessly give of their time and
talents to improve their communities.

FOREWORD

———

By Natalie Gochnour,
Associate Dean, David Eccles School of Business

Several years ago, I was caught off guard while attending a National Governors Association meeting in Indianapolis. At the time, I was a senior staff person for a governor. The governor asked me right before a governor-to-governor discussion if I had prepared any talking points about a local strategic planning endeavor. I didn't even know strategic planning was on the agenda and had about 10 minutes to get something prepared. I quickly put pen to paper.

I started my talking points with a simple phrase, "The best planning comes from the people." I then went on to capture the essence of community-based strategic planning.

I thought about this experience as I read *Elevating Trust in Local Government*. Community-based strategic planning is an expression of the peoples' wants and desires. It's not top down, it's bottom up. It's inclusive, flexible, and communicative. It's about the people's hopes and dreams for their community and how to make them happen.

I've learned over the course of my career that not only does the best planning come from the people, but there actually is a formula for success. And, I know of no better source for this formula than the ideas presented so accessibly in this book.

In kitchen-table English the authors share real-life stories about the advantages of strategic planning, the foundations for success, the obstacles, and applied tips about how to organize and pace a strategic planning effort. It reads as a "how-to" guide to create a strategic plan for your community.

Importantly, practitioners will learn how to involve agitated citizens, deal with misperceptions, prevail over organized opposition, and confront a lack of elected official or administrative support. They will also learn how to organize the process by forming an advisory committee, launching the effort, mapping the process, creating a mission statement and outline, and committing to a timeline.

The authors share many tips of the trade. They encourage leaders of a strategic planning effort to be flexible, be inclusive, not rush things, involve elected leaders, brand the effort, make revisions, keep an eye on execution, and make sure the work is ratified. By the end of the book the reader will not only recognize the power of community-based strategic planning, but will feel comfortable in executing a strategic planning process of their own.

I'm fond of the saying, "The future is not a gift, but an achievement." Indeed, we achieve beautiful, prosperous, and livable communities not by luck, but through our actions. This book will help elected officials, administrators, planners, and, most importantly, citizens act to achieve their highest aspirations for their community.

PREFACE

___

Congratulations! If you've picked up a copy of this book, it means you must be serious about planning for the future of your community. We hope you will find the perspective herein helpful in your strategic planning endeavors. We believe the process of engaging your community in development of a strategic plan can powerfully transform your impact and effectiveness.

As you flip through the pages of the book, you will notice that we rely on the first person to share our perspectives on community-based strategic planning. This is by design. Wherever you encounter the plural "we" means that both Dan and Rick are speaking from our collective experience. When you encounter "I", then one of us is speaking. To help you distinguish between the two, **Rick's anecdotes show up in bold letters.** *Dan's anecdotes show up in italics.*

Dan comes from a strategic planning background having facilitated hundreds of strategic planning endeavors with a variety of organizations ranging from large corporations to small non-profits to state agencies and municipal government. Rick has had a long career in municipal management and has presided over the strategic planning process in each of the communities where he has served as municipal manager as well as occasionally consulting with other communities relative to their strategic planning endeavors. We have attempted to weave together both perspectives to provide the reader with a solid practical understanding of strategic planning as well as how to apply that understanding in a municipal setting.

1

THE PARABLE OF THE CHICKEN SANDWICH

———

"You've got to be very careful if you don't know where you are going, because you might not get there."
— *Yogi Berra*

I could spend the first three chapters of this book making argument after argument as to why I believe planning strategically is simply the right thing to do for your community. More specifically, I could make the argument that strategic planning without input from those being served is in fact not planning at all. However, I have found very little that more vividly paints the picture as to why I feel so strongly about community-based strategic planning than the Parable of the Chicken Sandwich—a story derived from a singular experience on a family vacation. This parable is intended to teach a principle which I will describe at the conclusion of the story.

It had become a tradition that every year, commencing on the day following Christmas, my family would travel south into the Phoenix area to experience what we called our "end of year thaw." While it's 20°F during that time of year where we lived, it's usually 60°F in Arizona. It was during one of these excursions that I experienced what would later be dubbed the "Parable of the Chicken Sandwich."

Somewhere between Salt Lake City and Phoenix, there is an un-named, non-denominational fast food restaurant where we happened to stop for lunch. This was a typical fast food establishment with the usual fare of slightly less than healthy selections. My wife and three children ordered a hamburger and I ordered a chicken sandwich. That was my first mistake. I should've been one of the gang and simply ordered a hamburger. When the order was delivered to our table, I realized that all the sandwiches were in fact hamburgers. Rather than just sit there and consume the hamburger I did not order, I de-termined the best course of action was to return it and ask for my chicken sandwich.

When I approached the young lady behind the register, hamburger in hand, I politely informed her that I had mistakenly been given a hamburger and that I needed to exchange it for my original order, a chicken sandwich. Instead of executing my request, she turned around and walked behind the wall separating the dining area from the kitchen. I quickly reviewed in my mind everything I said to her in an effort to identify something potentially offensive. In very short order, a manager, or at least that's what his badge indicated, emerged and inquired regarding my "problem."

"No problem. I ordered a chicken sandwich and I was given a hamburger instead," I explained. "I just want to exchange it for a chicken sandwich." Taking the sandwich from my hand, he asked, "What's wrong with it?"

"Nothing," I answered. "It just isn't the thing that I ordered." With that explanation, I was confident that I had resolved the issue. I wondered what the young woman could have possibly told him in the back of the restaurant that would've given him any idea that this was anything beyond a simple error in filling a customer order.

"But it's perfectly good," he countered. At this point, I have to admit that his response was so unanticipated that for a split second I didn't know what to say. "I'm sure that it is," I replied, now agitated. "It's just that it isn't what I ordered."

With that, the manager threw the hamburger into an open trash receptacle, next to where they were serving food no less, and briskly grabbed a chicken sandwich from under the warmer, slapped it down on the counter in front of me, and walked away without saying a word. Before leaving, he flashed me one of those "unreasonable customer" looks. I didn't even feel like eating a chicken sandwich at that point. All I wanted to do was to get into the car and drive as far away as possible.

Now keep in mind that I had mentioned nothing about the quality of the sandwich, whether it was delicious, whether the bread was stale and vegetables limp. There are only two moving parts here. First, there is the mistaken delivery of my order, the hamburger, errantly provided instead of the chicken sandwich. However, even more egregious was the second part, the manager's shock and dismay associated with my complaint and the corresponding methodology he employed to "rectify" the situation.

When I relate this story to groupings of municipal officials, invariably there are many who appear appalled. Some even look as though they want to offer some type of condolence for the suffering I endured at the fast food establishment. However, the looks of sympathy quickly evaporate when I pose a very pointed question, "As absurd as this story sounds, how many of us are doing the same thing to our citizens?" What I'm trying to determine is whether we as elected and appointed municipal officials are providing our citizens with services that they neither requested nor particularly value.

As well-intentioned as we and our staffs are and regardless of the quality of the services we provide, it just might be that our citizens need, want, and expect something different. Sure, there are great numbers of citizens who accept the hamburger, eat it, and never utter a word of complaint. Then again, there are others who, despite our best efforts and intentions, are not happy with the direction of our local government; and just like the manager in the restaurant, we may even be prone to blame the citizens for their discontent. We may declare amongst ourselves, "We just aren't doing a very good job explaining the value of our services." Or we may say, "If they only knew about all of the effort, dedication, the blood sweat and tears poured into the community daily by our staff, they'd certainly have a different attitude."

Again, that's very much like the restaurant manager describing to me the quality of the products that went into making the hamburger . . . that I did not order. "But this hamburger is perfectly good," he had insisted. He completely disregarded the fact that I didn't order a hamburger. He completely ignored the fact that I had no desire for a hamburger and that I had already determined that a chicken sandwich would make me happier than a hamburger.

Our citizens may not clearly articulate it by themselves, but they know what makes up quality of life for them. They know why they moved to your community and they know what keeps them there. Our job is to discover this and then align our services with those expectations.

When I first visited Warsaw, Poland, I took a tour of the city. For those unfamiliar with the history, the Nazis leveled 85% of the city in 1944. Following the destruction, Stalin "liberated" the country and placed it under communist rule. Our tour guide shared that because the city had very few buildings still standing, Stalin decided to give a "gift" to the city. He constructed a massive tower right in the center of Warsaw. As of this writing, it is still the tallest building in Poland. The problem was that the Poles didn't want this building. They hadn't asked for it and didn't like it. It became a symbol of everything they hated about the Russians and communism.

While our city leaders may not do anything this dramatic, do we sometimes give "gifts" to our citizens that they don't really want? We may think we know what they want, but we won't truly know unless we ask them.

There are three powerful benefits associated with going through this type of exercise. First, as was already mentioned, citizens prefer to receive the services from their local government that best align with their concept of quality of life. However, beyond this, there are two other tremendous benefits associated with community-based strategic planning—fiscal and political.

Fiscal Benefits of Strategic Planning

No one would argue that we live in an era of increased scrutiny in government finances and operations. The Great Recession of 2008 ushered in a very different way of doing business that many in the city management profession labeled the "New Normal." The characteristics of the New Normal include not only elevated scrutiny, but also a corresponding call for greater transparency and accountability. Surely, you remember the battle cry "Do more with less!" And how about this one—"It's time to tighten our belt."

At the time the 2008 Recession struck, I was managing a city in Arizona, one of the hardest impacted states in the nation. Before it was over, I would lose one-third of my operating revenue. It was like the perfect storm. Not only were revenues hemorrhaging, but my elected officials were loath to place any additional burdens on citizens in order to make up lost revenue. To cap it off, they demanded that I not use one dollar of fund reserves.

I have to tell you, when you lose a third of your operating revenue, the only thing left to do is redraw the organizational chart and try your very best to preserve core services. We were able to get through it mostly because I had an excellent staff that turned over every leaf in an effort to save money. In addition, we had to let a lot of good people go. However, perhaps one of the most helpful things

in our corner during those difficult times was our community-based strategic plan. That plan allowed us to avoid placing resources in areas that simply weren't important to our residents. I am proud to say that unless you, as a resident of that town, lived at city hall or enjoyed watching local government as a hobby, you probably didn't know that the city was even struggling. That's because we were able to focus resources, as scarce as they were, on the things that were most important to our residents. This is not to say that the level of service remained the same as it was before the Recession. However, we were able to preserve the things that were most important. How would we have ever known to do that if we had not started with the very people being served?

In a Utah city I managed, we completed the strategic planning process near the end of my second year with that municipality. Prior to having a strategic plan, the elected officials met annually to determine the goals that they would impart to staff. The staff would then estimate in fiscal terms what they would need in order to realize those goals. It was a simple process, but one that certainly did not include public input. During my first budget cycle with this community, the elected officials identified several goals with an associated price tag of $3.1 million in new spending. By the midpoint of the second year, we had enough feedback from our strategic planning committee that we were able to articulate to our elected officials the things that were most important to citizens. The elected body used this feedback to compose their goals for that year. The results were astounding. New spending would be about $90,000. Mind you . . . this is in a community of 110,000 residents!

The reason the elected officials were able to move from over $3 million in new spending to less than $100,000 is mostly due to the fact that they knew what was most important to the citizens being served. The directives in the strategic plan left little room for doubt. Our citizens cared about community aesthetics, public safety, economic development, fiscal sustainability, parks and open space, and good infrastructure. That's it and that's all. Despite calls to the contrary from special interest groups, our citizens didn't expect our city to build a new art center or lavish recreation center. It astounded many of us that these kinds of things didn't even hit the radar during the planning process. What citizens wanted to make sure we had were things like enough cops on the street, enough money in the bank in case another rainy day should appear, and good roads.

There remains in every city the temptation to be all things to all people. We want our citizens to be happy; and like an all-too-typical parent, we think if we lavish them with things like elaborate libraries, aquatic centers, cultural and arts centers, etc., they will be happy, our elected officials will be reelected, and we will get a raise and perhaps even a commendation. In addition, many cities suffer from what we refer to as "Urban Manhood." This is a false notion which dictates that in order to be a "real" city, you have to have certain things in your community. These could include expensive community amenities like sports complexes, kitschy transit hubs, an urban style downtown, expensive municipal buildings (LEED certified of course) and a host of other things that may or may not be very important to the people that call your community home.

Now, please do not misunderstand. It may very well be that your citizens expect sports complexes, kitschy transit hubs, an urban style downtown, expensive municipal buildings, etc. However, how in the world are you ever going to know if you don't ask them? When we are confident about what our citizens expect, we are empowered to focus resources on those priorities and avoid wasting money on things that neither satisfy nor achieve any other end. Herein lies the principle promised at the beginning of this chapter.

Political Benefits of Strategic Planning

There are really two political benefits of strategic planning. The first pertains to political will and the second relates to the creation of community ownership. Both are critical.

Elected officials are regularly lobbied by small groups of business owners and residents demanding specific action. This may look like a group of soccer moms that demand that the city continue to build soccer fields. It may look like an arts council or group of theater people who demand that the city build a performing arts center. It may take the form of a developer who wants the city to invest in his or her project.

During that stint with my Arizona community, the city was approached by the local Native American tribe with the proposition of partnering to build a spring training facility for the Colorado Rockies and the Arizona Diamondbacks professional baseball clubs. The total cost of the project was $110 million. The tribe's role would be to provide the real estate for the facility, and the city would incur the debt associated with the development of the project. I quickly surmised that the annual debt service alone would equal our entire operating budget!

You have to understand that many communities in Arizona and in other locations throughout the country have a sincere desire to cooperate with and please their neighbors. Such was certainly the case in my city. Even though the project was completely and utterly infeasible for the city, elected officials deliberated over how they might pull a rabbit out of their hat and make this project work. The tribe had promised that the city could keep a portion of ticket sales and other concessionary revenue to offset the expense of the debt service. Meanwhile, they argued the facility would draw additional economic development to the area that would further benefit the city. I and our staff provided the necessary analysis and determined that revenues from the facility would come nowhere near providing even a fraction of the funding necessary to service the debt. We additionally looked at the possibilities for economic development and calculated an appropriate multiplier effect. Again, a big fat loser! Regardless, the elected officials did not want to return to the tribal council and tell them that the city would not participate. I recall their discussing how they would explain the fact that the city simply did not have the money to build such a facility.

That's when one of our elected officials held up a copy of our strategic plan and said, "You know, there's not one thing in our strategic plan that relates in the least to a spring training facility." With that, the elected body determined that they would authorize the mayor to sit down with the president of the tribe and explain the misalignment between this particular project and the priorities of the citizens. All this having been done, the relationship between the mayor and the president of the tribe was preserved; mostly because the president clearly understood the problem associated with spending money on something that was not a priority of the people. I have contemplated many times what would've happened had our elected officials not taken the time to understand community priorities. Therein lies the magic.

> **A strategic plan provides policy makers with the discipline and will to say yes to those opportunities that align with community priorities and the discipline and will to say no to those that don't.**

Finally, local governments that take the time to include citizens in strategic planning are most likely to instill a sense of ownership on the part of those participating in the creation of the plan. Community ownership, meanwhile, is a common characteristic of people who are happy with their local government. Conversely, people become agitated when they feel that they have been disenfranchised or when they believe that their local government has become disengaged.

OTHER PRACTICAL REASONS

I recall one occasion visiting a small Alaskan city where I was assisting that municipality with a performance analysis of their organization. During the early stages of that evaluation, I sat in a conference room with the municipal manager, the assistant manager, and a host of other department heads. One of the questions that I nearly always pose to a city is whether they have a community strategic plan. Go figure. I think the manager already anticipated that I was going to ask this question because before I could even get the question out of my mouth, he reached behind and grabbed a large, bound document from a bookcase.

Plopping it on the table, he exclaimed, "There it is." I took a moment while one of my colleagues continued asking questions to thumb through this rather voluminous piece of work. Clearly, a lot of thought, at least someone's thought, went into the composition of this book. It had charts, analyses, scatterplots, tables, and every other thing one would expect to see in a corporate-style strategic plan. It had pretty pictures, glossy pages, the works. This was someone's masterpiece. I found an opportune time to return to the subject by asking whether the elected body had adopted this plan. I was quickly assured that the elected body, seven years prior, had officially ratified it. Then I asked a Dr. Phil question, "So how's that working out for you?" The assistant manager was the first to speak up after a slightly awkward pause. "Not very well." I asked why not, to which he answered, "Because nobody uses it." He described how the plan, after its adoption, was immediately banished to the shelf on the bookcase inside that very conference room. No one refers to it and few have ever read it. I asked him and everyone else in the room why they thought the plan had never been implemented. No one had a particularly clear answer, but the assistant conjectured, "It's probably because no one ever thought of how they were going to implement it when they created it."

I thought this might be the appropriate time for a little bit of education. As I often do, I led with a question, "Who composed this plan?" The answer was quick, "We did." When I probed a little deeper into what "we" meant, he described that the plan was the product of administration and department heads contributing sections to the plan. I

asked if anyone had taken any time to consult with citizens, stakeholder groups, the neighboring native tribe, businesses, the school district, etc. No, no, no, no, and no were their answers. I then explained to them this principle: you exponentially increase the survivability of any plan when you expand the base of participation in creating it. You can go too far with any good thing, but we rarely find communities where the city has done too much to expand the base of participation. Inviting the input of your citizens and stakeholder groups in the creation of a plan that directly impacts their community nearly always results in a greater likelihood that the plan will be implemented and that it will survive changes in administration and political leadership.

You are more likely to come to the correct conclusions and implement the right ideas if you take the opportunity to synergize your problem-solving efforts with your citizens. The International City and County Management Association (ICMA) in their article "Citizen Engagement: An Outgrowth of Civic Awareness" put it this way:

"Communities that take the time to educate their residents and then offer them the opportunity to participate in activities such as local strategic planning and financial decision making are undoubtedly more likely to experience greater success in these areas."[1]

Concerning this mutual participation, and here I'll take a page from Steven R. Covey, synergy is a principal that is best described with the mathematical equation $1+1 = 3$. It means that when we combine our problem-solving abilities with others, we are most likely to arrive at a solution that is better than the one that we would have developed alone. However, the folks in Alaska may have answered this with, "But we had a lot of people around the table helping us put this plan together. Isn't that synergy?" Our answer is that the critical question does not revolve around how many individuals you involve in creating a plan, but in how

---

[1] ICMA (International City and County Management Association). "Citizen Engagement: An Outgrowth of Civic Awareness." Published September 17, 2010, https://icma.org/articles/article/citizen-engagement-outgrowth-civic-awareness.

many different perspectives you have involved. That was a critical component missing in the composition of that community's strategic plan. This element may be missing from your own plan. If it is, that's okay.

Not too long ago I was asked by a Colorado community whether I thought they ought to trash their current plan in favor of beginning a community-based plan. Again, leading with a question, I asked another Dr. Phil: "How's the plan working out for you?" They said that they thought things were working well in their community. Surveys indicated that citizens were happy with the level of service they were providing and that the city was heading in the right direction. I advised them not to "throw the baby out with the bathwater." Rather, I counseled them to begin engaging citizens and stakeholder groups when next they updated the plan.

I don't know of a single manager out there who would not be thinking at this point, "Great. I can hardly get my elected officials to agree on annual goals, much less get the whole community on the same page." I have been there. In my first annual retreat, I listed nearly 100 separate programs and services that we were offering. I then allotted a number of red, yellow, green, and blue dots to my elected officials at our annual retreat and asked them to prioritize programs and services with their dots. The color red indicated that they wanted to see something change or improved, yellow indicated that we needed to continue to monitor and possibly address a particular program or service, green indicated satisfaction with the direction of that program or service, and blue was kind of a default color which communicated, "Why in the heck are we even doing this?" That is what I used to call strategic planning. I figured that if citizens didn't like it, they could let their elected officials know.

We're not going to lie to you and tell you that "the dot exercise" isn't a whole lot easier than community-based strategic planning. However, once you have gone through a community-based strategic planning process, it will not only become part of your nature and make you more effective when you revise the plan, but you will discover a clarity and power that you have not enjoyed before. This book is intended to help you make that process as smooth and enjoyable as possible.

CONCLUSION

Our cities, towns, counties, and districts are generally staffed with competent and well-intentioned public servants. Nevertheless, citizens may feel a disconnection with local government if they believe they are not receiving the municipal services they expect in order to enjoy a high quality of life. Successfully providing the services citizens desire is a process that begins with asking them what they expect from their local government. Such a process not only connects citizens with local governance, but also provides other benefits. For example, since community-based strategic planning reveals those priorities of most importance to citizens, municipalities can focus finite resources on those things that matter most, facilitating the identification of those initiatives, programs, and services that are not aligned with the expectations and desires of the citizenry. A community-based plan can also provide policymakers with the ability to place the rhetoric and lobbying of special interest groups in perspective. Meanwhile, community cohesiveness and a sense of ownership are created as those being served are invited to participate in the identification of community priorities. Broadening the base of participation in creating the strategic plan increases the likelihood that it will not only be used but also survive administrative and political leadership changes and transitions.

TAKEAWAYS

» *As well-intentioned as municipal staff and elected officials may be and regardless of the quality of the services provided, it just could be that our citizens need, want, and expect something different.*

» *Our citizens may not clearly articulate it by themselves, but they know what makes up quality of life for them. They know why they moved to your community and they know what keeps them there. Our job is to discover this and then align our services with those expectations.*

» *When we are confident about what our citizens expect, we are empowered to focus resources on those priorities and avoid spending money on programs outside of those expectations.*

» *A strategic plan provides policy makers with the will to say "yes" to those opportunities that align with community priorities and the discipline to say "no" to those that don't.*

» *Local governments that take the time to include citizens in strategic planning are most likely to instill a sense of shared ownership. Community ownership, meanwhile, is a common characteristic of people who are happy with their local government.*

» *Inviting the input of your citizens and stakeholder groups in the creation of a plan that directly impacts their community nearly always results in a greater likelihood that the plan will be implemented and that it will survive changes in administration and political leadership.*

2

SETTING THE FOUNDATION

---

*"Absolute identity with one's cause is the first and
great condition of successful leadership."*
—*Woodrow Wilson*

Not too long ago, I was presenting a session at the Utah League of Cities and Towns annual conference in St. George, Utah. As kind of an icebreaker and way to open up the subject of strategic planning with the audience, mostly composed of elected officials, I posed the question: "How many of you believe that you know your citizens well enough to know what they need?" About half of the hands went up. I think this belief or idea is very common among elected officials, especially in some of our smaller communities where everybody knows their neighbor and everyone else in town. I then posed the second question: "How many of you who just raised your hand sometimes have trouble figuring out what your spouse or children need or want?" Not surprisingly, the same hands were raised. I then posed my third and entirely rhetorical question, "If you have trouble figuring out what your family needs and expects, how in the

world can you be confident that you know what your citizens expect and need?"

We don't know of too many people who run for public office or aspire to high administrative office who don't think of themselves as leaders. Most are well-intentioned people who believe that they have a lot to bring to their community and want to lead people to some better place. Others may be driven to obtain leadership positions by other motivators, such as a need for recognition, eventual higher office, status, and even wealth. Our experience has been that in general, the latter group is considerably less interested in finding out what citizens want because they are most interested in getting citizens to conform to what <u>they</u> want. For the majority in this camp, their ascension to power reinforces in their own minds their capability and even responsibility to determine the needs of those over whom they preside. Mother knows best.

This is not to say that everyone who raised their hand in the Utah session were egotistical, self-glorifying megalomaniacs. They, and perhaps many reading this book, may suffer from a misimpression that to be a leader you have to act; you have to be the one to lead out; you have to be a Kaiser, a general. After all, leaders don't have time to poll every one of their troops before they march into battle. You can't be a lilting daisy and be a leader. You must show iron, resolve, and decisiveness. Then again, many in the audience may simply believe they've known their people long enough that they are familiar with what makes them tick.

We began our journey of discovery with this discussion because an examination of current leadership attitudes and motivators is fundamental to beginning a strategic planning process. Strategic planning is a leadership-driven initiative. There is little to be gained from the exercise unless the political and organizational leaders support the process and then have the will to do whatever it takes to make policy and align resources with the directives of the plan.

Jim Collins, a best-selling author who brought us one of the most important books on management entitled Good to Great, has spent decades researching highly successful organizations to identify those characteristics that enabled them to move from mediocrity to greatness. One of the key characteristics is captured in the concept known as the "Level 5 Leader."

This type of leader, according to Collins, captures all of the characteristics of lower rung leaders. For example, they are highly capable, contributing team members, competent managers, and effective leaders. However, Level 5 Leaders add to this array with the capability of building enduring greatness "through a paradoxical blend of *personal humility and professional will.*"[2]

And lest we think that Level 5 Leadership is a critical element leading to greatness in exclusively *private* sector organizations, Collins authored a follow-up booklet entitled *Good to Great and the Social Sectors.* In that 35-page complement to his larger, more private-sector oriented book, Collins makes it very clear that Level 5 Leadership is just as critical in the public sector as it is the private sector. He specifically states, "In legislative leadership, on the other hand, no individual leader—not even the nominal chief executive—has enough structural power to make the most important decisions by himself or herself. Legislative leadership relies more upon persuasion, political currency, and shared interest to create the conditions for the right decisions to happen. And it is precisely this legislative dynamic that makes Level 5 Leadership particularly important to the social sectors."[3]

But exactly how does Level 5 Leadership relate to community-based strategic planning? To provide an adequate answer, let's delve a little deeper into "personal humility and professional will."

I was once asked by a very sincere and newly elected council member what characteristic she could bring to our governing body

[2] Jim Collins, Good to Great (New York: HarperBusiness, 2001), 20.

[3] Jim Collins, *Good to Great and the Social Sectors: Why Business Thinking Is Not the Answer* (Boulder, Colo.: Jim Collins, 2005), 11.

that would be of most value to her colleagues and to me as an administrator. It didn't take me long to answer. "Personal humility," I answered. I went on to explain to this elected official that our organization's lifeblood was trust. I said that she needed to know that her new organization at city hall was composed of hundreds of very dedicated public servants and an array of department heads with centuries of combined experience. I told her that as an elected official she deserved the respect and dignity tied to her office, but I also told her that it would be critically important for her to understand that she was not going to be able to approximate the level of expertise and experience possessed by our staff. I advised her to be inquisitive, be watchful, be curious, be teachable, and learn. However, I promised her that if she would demonstrate trust and personal humility, our staff would demonstrate dedication, competence, and trustworthiness.

Personal humility is a strength exhibited by capable leaders who recognize that they do not have the answer to every question. They recognize that part of leadership entails involving those whom they serve in crafting a vision. Personal humility allows leaders to ask questions, to observe and learn, all without feeling like they've abdicated their leadership role and responsibilities. In Doris Kearns Goodwin's "Team of Rivals," she points to Abraham Lincoln's ability to subject his personal feelings and ego to the more important task of assembling a cabinet composed of the most capable individuals. As Goodwin notes, Lincoln's cabinet was made-up of several individuals who had been political rivals and indeed harshly critical of the President before his election.[4] Lincoln knew that he could not be successful in preserving the Union by himself. He embraced the reality that he needed others, and he valued specifically the input from those whose perspectives were significantly different from

---

[4] Doris Kearns Goodwin, *Team of Rivals: The Political Genius of Abraham Lincoln* (New York: Simon & Schuster, 2005).

his own. Personality and even political differences were not as important to Lincoln because he and his cabinet members shared a fundamental dedication to preserving the Union.

Thus, when personal humility is woven into the fabric of our character as local government officials, it becomes comfortable and even desirable to ask the people we serve what they think, what they hope for, and what they would do in our place. And we can ask these questions without feeling like we have abdicated our offices. Ironically, personal humility allows us to become more confident in the positions that we take and the policies we prescribe.

The paradoxical companion of personal humility, as such applies to leadership, is professional will. Level 5 Leaders demonstrate exceptional drive and dedication to the realization of their organizational mission. To these types of leaders, personal needs are subordinated to the needs of the organization and its mission. Harry Truman was fond of saying, "It is amazing what you can accomplish if you do not care who gets the credit."[5] For community-based strategic planning to be effective, political and organizational leaders need to embrace the prospect of implementing somebody else's ideas. At the end of the strategic planning process, you are going to be left with an array of directives and initiatives that did not necessarily have their genesis in your own set of gray matter. This is going to be the citizens' plan. Yours will be the responsibility for making sure that it is effectively implemented. In order for it to be effectively put into action, you and others that compose the leadership infrastructure of your community must demonstrate an unwavering and singular dedication to realizing the vision articulated by your citizens.

If you can bring both personal humility and professional will to the strategic planning process and to the eventual implementation of your plan, you will have accomplished something that few communities have. According to an ICMA 2009 survey, only about 62% of communities admit

---

[5] Harry S. Truman (1884–1972).

to having a strategic plan. Smaller governments are less likely to have a strategic plan, while council-manager led organizations are most likely to have one. Meanwhile, only about 77% of communities with strategic plans link them to their allocation of resources. However, what is most astounding is that of those communities with strategic plans, only 29% of them involved their citizens in resource allocation decisions.[6]

It's clear that most communities believe it is important to have some type of roadmap, vision, or plan. But the vast majority have not gone so far as to involve the people being served in the strategic planning process. It isn't that the idea is so foreign to these organizations. There are a variety of reasons why perhaps well-intentioned municipalities have opted not to involve citizens. **I once asked one of my colleagues in Utah about his strategic planning process. When the conversation touched on citizen involvement, he said, "It's not that we haven't involved our citizens. We have actually from time to time asked their opinions, but we have not found it to be a particularly productive exercise." This led me to contemplate what exactly my colleagues, otherwise very capable administrators and officials, are experiencing that has dissuaded them from fully involving their citizens in the strategic planning process.**

We have identified four fundamental obstacles to strategic planning. In describing these obstacles, we will also offer some advice on overcoming them. They are:

>   *A lack of elected official and/or administrative support*

>   *An agitated citizenry*

>   *Organizational resistance*

>   *Misperceptions about strategic planning*

---

[6] ICMA: State of the Profession Survey, 2009.

Lack of Elected Official and Administrative Support

If you're reading this book, we're going to assume for argument's sake that you're interested in pursuing a community-based strategic planning initiative for your local government. You may already see the value that such a plan could represent. However, your perspective may not be shared by some of your elected officials and the municipality's administration. While there may be hundreds of reasons for this, let's focus on the most likely factors generating internal opposition to a strategic planning endeavor.

First and foremost, human beings, in their primal default mode, are not prone to embrace change. We tend to be creatures of habit and regimen. We are likewise skeptical of anything that appears to break with routine. It is not uncommon for members of the elected body and the administration to become comfortable with their situations. In the absence of pain itself, there may not be any motivators strong enough to inspire action. "If it ain't broke, don't fix it" is what you're going to hear from individuals who are settled into a status quo and "steady as she goes" mode. No doubt you are going to encounter individuals who are near the end of their term or career and prefer not to rock the boat.

Our advice is to take their inhibitions and concerns very seriously. It's not that your colleagues are "sticks in the mud," as much as they are human. Many communities have existed with very little change over the decades and even centuries. There may be people within your organization, meanwhile, who have served there for decades. One of the most common mistakes that change agents make is assuming that if people intellectually understand the concept you are promoting, they are ready for change. In his book *Managing at the Speed of Change*, Daryl Conner explains that "intellectual preparation cannot be confused with emotional readiness." He points out that the human mind can process data much faster than the heart can.[7] The premise here is that any change needs to be absorbed, understood, embraced, and digested both intellectually *and* emotionally before change can be implemented. If your community is not accustomed to asking for public input, the idea of basing your entire strategic plan on what citizens have to say is apt to make a lot of people inside your local government pretty nervous.

Our next piece of advice is to take it slow. If your community already has a strategic plan, follow the advice we gave to that Colorado community mentioned earlier. Don't throw the baby out with the bathwater. You may want to start by asking some questions: "How effectively have we implemented our strategic plan?" "How can we improve our next planning endeavor by including our citizens in the process?" You may be surprised by what you hear. You may discover that your administration diligently tracks the implementation of your strategic plan with the use of performance outcomes. (We will discuss performance outcomes in greater detail later in the book.) You may also find that like the Alaskan community we mentioned, significant elements of the plan have never been implemented. Maybe your plan is simply sitting on a shelf collecting dust. You won't know until you ask. In response to the second question about including your citizens in the process, you may receive some grins and chuckles. Again, if your organization is like Rick's colleague's in Utah, it may be that you've tried to solicit citizen participation in planning but with limited success.

All of this is okay. The most important thing is to break the ice. Our experience is that questions like these are best posed at annual goal-setting retreats or in one-on-one conversations with colleagues. The critical advice here is to go slow and allow people to react to the idea. Remember that even more important than understanding the reasons for and the process associated with strategic planning is the emotional

---

[7] Daryl R. Connor, *Managing at the Speed of Change: How Resilient Managers Succeed and Prosper Where Others Fail* (New York: Villard Books, 1993), 22, 25.

readiness to embrace it. Leadership is all about taking people to places that they want to go anyway. It's about allowing people to follow when they have the choice not to. Leadership cannot exist in the same space as coercion or force, even if the leader believes he or she is acting in the best interests of the community. We have worked with communities who immediately embrace the idea of community-based strategic planning and others who have taken months and even years to warm up to the idea.

You may find that many staff and elected officials are feeling some trepidation in asking questions when they don't already know what the answers are. Asking citizens what they believe is important and what they want from their local government can be scary. What if we don't have the means of providing what they want? Perhaps it's better if we don't ask at all. It is true that if you ask citizens to help you put together a blueprint and vision for their community, you're going to have to be ready to act on the input you receive. That is simply a very intimidating realization to a lot of officials.

This is a very natural reaction to the unknown. Our advice is to avoid downplaying this fear or making people feel silly or uncaring because they're afraid to ask for input. We have been through some very turbulent times. Citizen feelings of disengagement appear to be relatively high. Meanwhile, citizen trust in your community may be low. Asking for input in these times can certainly be viewed as an invitation to be punched in the gut. In fact, some officials may fear that the relationship between government and the governed is so bad that they won't receive any constructive feedback at all. The best course to take if you encounter opposition like this is to acknowledge what they're feeling and attempt to counter it by articulating the reality that the reason many citizens feel disengaged from their local government is that we commonly *don't* ask for their involvement and input. Try to explain that trust is certainly not going to be the product of continuing to exclude citizens from the planning process. Trust begets trust. When we reach out to our citizens and involve them in creating a vision for their future, then follow through on that plan, trust is going to be the byproduct. You may sense that asking angry citizens what their local government ought to be doing to improve their lives is akin to giving a mob pitchforks and torches. Why pour gasoline on a fire? In addition, what if they do ask for the absurd, unaffordable, and the infeasible?

Remember this important point: If your base of participation in the strategic planning process is broad enough, extreme and/or hostile voices tend to blend into the sounds of a larger symphony of reason. *As a part of a strategic planning exercise that I facilitated for a large suburban community, I experienced that hostility first-hand during a community dialogue session. For this particular community, we ran several such dialogue sessions. Most were very productive with citizens expressing concerns, hopes for the future, and leaving with a shared sense that they had just been part of shaping the future of their community. For the final session, two residents came with a very visible chip on their shoulders. Despite my best efforts to lay out the purpose of the meeting, they were intent on hijacking a portion of the meeting so that they could offer up their opinions on the upcoming national elections and national ideological issues that had no bearing on the community-based strategic planning process. They were some of the first to leave the meeting when we concluded. As I spoke with other residents after the meeting, they offered their apologies by saying things like, "We really do have good people here in our community. While there may be a few naysayers, we're so grateful that our local government is creating opportunities for residents to participate in planning for the future of our community."*

Of course you're going to hear from what one attorney friend of ours used to call "the crazy angries." When residents show up to a meeting after spending hours listening to Sean Hannity or Rachel Maddow, naturally, you're going to hear that kind of commentary. Every community enjoys the presence of a few very vocal and agitated citizens. More on this later. However, when your citizens speak as a larger voice, you will be both surprised and not surprised. You will be surprised at how reasonable, logical, and constructive the feedback is. You will *not* be surprised at the list of qualities, services, and characteristics your citizens believe crucial to quality of life. In fact, we commonly point out that if the strategic directives developed by your strategic planning committee surprise you, either you didn't do a good job in interpreting citizen feedback or you've been very much out of touch with your citizens. Therefore, try to put your colleagues at ease by assuring them that your citizens are reasonable and like you, want the very best for their community.

Meanwhile, it may be that your citizens *do* voice a desire for something that you have deemed unaffordable or infeasible in the present. Ignoring this desire is not going to make it go away, and pretending that it never existed is also not a rational course of action. In yet another community, it was discovered that citizens placed the construction of a recreation center at the top of their list. Meeting with the municipal manager, he expressed his frustration over the possibility of now having to find the funding for a project that he believed completely unaffordable. He said, "If the citizens knew how much that would affect their property tax, I don't think you'd see as much enthusiasm for it." Rick assured him that he believed his citizens *would* understand the fiscal implications of building a new recreation center, but he also added, "What the citizens *will not* understand is why their municipality would be willing to ignore what they perceive to be a very real need in the community."

Regardless of what appears feasible or infeasible at the moment, an articulated community priority provides your local government with the opportunity to acquaint your citizens with the process of planning for such an amenity, facility, or program. Citizens don't expect us to just run out and bond for millions of dollars. However, they *do* expect us to acknowledge the need and begin planning for the day when such a project can become a reality.

Going back to an earlier point, some members of the elected body and even in the administrator's office may feel that going through a community-based strategic planning process is similar to admitting that they've never known what they were doing before the process. Some may feel that starting something like this appears to citizens like officials are abdicating their positions. Asking citizens what they think may make them look weak and indecisive; and they may even fear that they will be accused of "leading through polls."

We have never been involved in a strategic planning process where citizens did not profusely thank and compliment their elected body for reaching out to them for their input. If you face an obstacle like this, it's best not to refute or argue. Acknowledge the possibility and likelihood that *whatever* your officials do is likely to draw criticism from some corner of your community. However, assure them that the vast majority of your citizens will be grateful for the opportunity to reengage with their local government.

Lastly, officials may not perceive any real value that can be derived from the community-based strategic planning process. This is particularly common in the administrative office. They generally feel that the community is steaming ahead in the right direction and they don't want to mess up the journey by asking the citizens about their preferred destination. Many managers, particularly, feel like they have enjoyed a significant track record of making the right decisions for the community without such a citizen-based plan, and they cannot understand how such a plan will aid them in making better decisions.

Municipal managers may need to be reminded that elected officials often require tools necessary to do their jobs as policymakers that managers do not necessarily need. Managers are facilitators and implementers. They are not policymakers in a legislative sense. Therefore, it is best that managers remember that their elected body will make the best decisions and policies if they have the appropriate tools. In the end, the manager and his staff are going to be very real beneficiaries of the process. Allow us to provide an example.

We, as perhaps you, have sat through hours of debate at annual goal setting retreats regarding what the coming year's priorities ought to be. **For many communities, this debate may span two full days, as was the case in one community I managed before we could assemble a strategic plan. After we had the plan, I could shave hours off of the process. The reason the retreat became a shorter experience is because the elected officials already began with an understanding of what community priorities were. This doesn't mean they weren't free to discuss situations and functions unarticulated in our strategic plan; but when it came to setting the goals for the following year, the process became much smoother. In addition, having a long-range strategic plan and goals from the elected body for the current year allowed the staff to streamline the budget process. Every year, following the goal-setting retreat, I held a department head or cabinet retreat. At this meeting, we would take a day, strategic plan and goals in hand, to compose the business plan for the next fiscal year, which served as the basis for budget requests. This process allowed us to eliminate a lot of the jockeying, positioning, and lobbying that had become commonplace in the organization. We all knew what the community priorities were and we knew that the goals from the elected body reflected those.** We will describe this process in greater detail later in the book.

Therefore, if you face this type of opposition, try to describe to those who share this concern how their jobs and lives are going to become better with the added clarity that a community-based strategic plan provides. You can do this while not taking anything away from the accomplishments your manager or staff have realized. Explain that this is a tool to help elected policymakers do *their* job with more confidence, clarity, and political will. Explain that the byproduct of this process is likely to be facilitated goal-setting and a smoother budget process, both of which will make their jobs and lives a lot easier.

An Agitated Citizenry

I remember that I was on my way to work one morning when I first heard on the radio about a movement called the "Tea Party." Like many Americans at the time and certainly now, I was and remain very concerned about the level of federal spending and our growing national debt. I used to wonder why our government in Washington couldn't balance its budget the way we cities were required to. All municipal governments are required to balance their budgets every year. Not to be too cavalier, because I would certainly like to print my own local money the way the federal government prints their money. I can see why they find it attractive, but the reality is that my expenses and revenues balance every year.

Without that money printing option at my disposal, I therefore identified and sympathized with the millions of Americans who wanted to return to an era of more fiscally responsible government—and more responsive and accountable government also. I remember thinking to myself how clever it was to capture and present growing public concern about the management of our federal government in a way that was tied to one of the most pivotal events leading to our national revolution. I pictured in my mind a scene of Mohawk-clad citizens throwing chests of federal spending and debt into the Boston Harbor.

I was very much attracted to the Tea Party cause. Who wouldn't want limited federal intrusion, a sounder economy, less debt, etc.? However, as things evolved, the rhetoric coming from some claiming to be part of this movement appeared to more hostile. Before long, I perceived much of what some were calling for was not just limited government, but no government. At the same time, criticism of the federal government expanded to very harsh critiques of all levels of government, including local governments.

Unfortunately, cities such as San Bernardino, Detroit, and Bell were throwing a lot of chum into the water via their alleged mismanagement. By 2010, we found that what began as a clever way of voicing popular concern about federal fiscal practices had, on some fronts, morphed into a general hostility toward all levels of government. It was surprising how quickly some people drew parallels between what the president or Congress was doing or espousing and what was happening at city hall, the county courthouse, or their local school board. Likewise, if right or left-wing pundits said Washington was out of control and spending recklessly, it was so at the local level as well, at least in the minds of many.

Fast-forward a few years and we still suffer from a disconnection between government and the governed. The economy may have come back, but trust has been left at the depot. Citizens don't trust government and I am sad to say that many in local government don't trust some of our citizens. There are meanwhile very few communities that enjoy little more than an unsettled and unfortunately very temporary political calm. It's very much like a demilitarized zone in some communities, where there may not be any metaphorical shooting for the moment, but enemies have their eyes locked on each other, waiting for the next municipal election before political holy terror breaks out. Now, you may say that this disconnect has always been there, that people have always distrusted government. However, we don't recall a period of time when citizens have been more agitated and at least appear to be more prone to distrust. Meanwhile, for many in the municipal management profession, survival strategies have called for hunkering down and riding out the storm of public discontent. In fact, at the time of this writing, we can sincerely say that we don't recall an era in the past three decades where we have seen more administrators and even elected officials so unsettled and just plain nervous. They're not so nervous about the economy, shrinking transportation dollars, growing homelessness, or any other array of concerns that usually hit the radar of municipal officials. No, many are afraid that if they show the least degree of out-of-the-box thinking, anything novel or progressive, somebody's going to come out of the woodwork and put a hammer right in the middle of their foreheads, politically speaking.

We used to call political landmines "rakes in the grass." Hopefully you've never had this happen to you before. You're walking along in your yard and you inadvertently step on the teeth of a rake concealed in your grass. The weight of your foot on the rake propels the wooden handle forward until it strikes you between your eyes. **Allow me to share an example of one such rake that nearly struck me.**

City Hall was a magnificent facility of more than 60,000 square feet, a noble structure with pillars and a clock tower. It was the most "municipal" looking structure I had ever seen. The more than two acres of landscaping surrounding this building however looked much like something from *The Addams Family*. Trying to describe the scene here would not do it justice, but take my word for it . . . somebody without a whole lot of talent in horticulture and landscape design had once upon a time prescribed that entire horrible scene. There was very little turf, a lot of scraggly xeriscape (low water use) plant species, rocks, and quite a few bushes that simply looked like milkweeds.

Within a year after assuming my duties, I met with our parks superintendent who walked the property with me and was eager to share some ideas he and his crew had with regard to our landscaping. He told me that the current configuration actually caused more maintenance and was harder on the irrigation infrastructure than anything one could possibly place on that property. He suggested to me that it would be helpful to allow one of our parks employees, who dabbled in landscape design, to develop a comprehensive and new schematic for city hall landscaping. I agreed to allow our employee to develop a plan on city time, and I agreed further to look over the plan with our superintendent when it was completed.

A few weeks passed and the superintendent was back at my office with the employee who had designed a new landscape for our municipal edifice. We unrolled the drawings on a conference table, and I have to say that I was very impressed. I thought to myself, "Now this is what our landscape ought to look like." I was concerned about

the way our property looked because we were planning a redevelopment of our downtown, and our city building would certainly be one of the anchors of this redevelopment endeavor. If we couldn't improve the aesthetics of City Hall, I feared that it might discourage developer interests in the project.

I complimented the plan and even went so far as to say that I wanted to show it to the council. I made plans to take the issue up with our elected officials at the next work meeting. In fact, I invited our superintendent and parks employee who designed the new landscape to attend with me and assist in making the presentation. Meanwhile, I asked the superintendent to put together some possible budgetary numbers that would go along with reworking the landscaping. I was very encouraged when the numbers came in well within reason, and I was confident the council would see the wisdom in shaping-up the appearance of our primary municipal building. They did indeed. I think it was easy for them to see the benefits of the project, and they were quick to lend their support. Since the budget process was underway, I began to make plans to include these costs as part of the annual budget.

That's when I noticed our clerk, a lifelong resident and longtime employee, behaving more strangely than usual. I told her that I noticed that she didn't seem to be her old self and I asked if there was anything wrong. Now mind you, she wasn't behaving in a depressed or downtrodden manner. She just had a persistent look on her face similar to the kind people wear when they know they're about to see two trains collide. After some prodding and encouragement, she finally opened up, "Do you know how much controversy surrounded the re-landscaping of our building years ago?" she asked. "Re-landscape?" I said countering the question with a question. She then proceeded to tell me the story of how when city hall was constructed, the landscaping was composed almost entirely of trees and turf. A few years later, elected officials at that time decided to set a water-wise example and xeriscape city hall at a cost of more than $300,000! Our clerk then told me that rumors of recall elections and investigations emerged as a result of that re-landscaping. According to her, the entire community was thrown into a tailspin.

She then told me further that word had already found its way onto the streets (gee, I wonder how . . .) about my intentions to re-landscape the building. She told me that several prominent and very active citizens were already gathering their troops and assembling petitions. There was no way in Haiti that they were going to allow me to do more landscaping at city hall. I quickly met with our elected officials and told them, after my own investigative work confirming what our clerk had said, that it might not be the best time to bring the subject of landscaping to the forefront or even the backside of our budget process. They also saw the light, recognized the rake in the grass, and we all decided to just walk away from the subject for the time being. Over the following years, after community aesthetics and specifically the appearance of our city hall emerged as priorities in our strategic plan, we would address landscaping in a measured manner.

The consequences associated with not paying attention to the "subtle" signals being provided by our clerk could have been un-fortunate. That community had already burned through more than a half-dozen managers in less than 18 years. It knew how to make management changes. Now, if you're thinking that the point of this story is that in order to survive as a municipal manager, you need to know when to landscape and when to just leave it alone, you missed it. The point is that your community is perhaps littered with more rakes in the grass (political hot topics and nuclear buttons) than maybe any other time in its history, and the number of these landmines could be increasing. If they are, they may be increasing partly because of a disconnect between government and citizens. Popular media culture has done its share of fanning the fires of public discontent. However, what are the real reasons for this divide and plethora of yard tools in the grass?

Surely we are better able to address this condition if we know what brought us to where we are. Despite what we stated earlier, the Tea Party didn't cause this. Hannity and Palin didn't cause this. Overzealous water conservationists didn't cause this. In Rick's story and example, people were not becoming upset because of his plans to plant more turf and trees around city hall. And we were so early in the process, that the costs of such landscaping were generally unknown. No, they were angry because *they didn't trust their local government with this decision.* They did not believe that anyone inside that grand edifice cared in the very least that the money that they were spending was in fact not theirs.

We have found that there is a natural righteous indignation that ignites within most people when they believe that they are being taken advantage of or when they are convinced that they are being taken for a ride without their consent. Not only is it *their* money that we were going to spend, but many of these angry citizens didn't feel like they enjoyed any ownership in the solution being proposed. It's kind of like asking you for your wallet and telling you of our intent to buy something with your money at the store. When you naturally ask what we are going to buy, we simply tell you not to worry about it and assure you that you will like what we purchase. After not too many events like this, of course, you're going to have your guard up every time you see us. "They're going to ask me for my wallet again; and they're going to go to the store and buy who knows what, pat me on the head, and tell me that I will like it." Here's hoping that your spouse doesn't treat you this way.

That's the real reason why there sometimes exists a disconnect between local government and citizens. Even the Declaration of Independence references the fact that government draws its power from the *consent* of the governed, and many citizens (and we see this in every community) believe that they should be able to consent and provide other input beyond simply casting a ballot at election time. They believe that they should continue to have a voice in their community *after* Election Day. Unfortunately, many do not feel that even their local government is theirs anymore. A citizen once told us, "I feel the same way about our community as I did when my brothers used to play keep-away," he said. "No matter how hard I tried to touch the ball, they would throw it around me, between my legs, and over my head. Every election, we citizens just select new people to keep the ball away from us."

A recent Gallup poll shows that 71% of Americans are dissatisfied with the nation's system of government and how well it works, the highest percentage since 2001. Actually, Gallup shows that dissatisfaction has been in a state of serious decline for the past two decades.[8] Perhaps a little good news for those in local government is that people tend to trust their municipality more than any other level of government. A very recent Gallup poll shows that 71% of Americans have a great deal to a fair amount of confidence in their local government. A little unnerving is the reality that this percentage has changed precious little for the last 40 years. In fact, the highest level of local government confidence shown in a Gallup poll reached 77% in December 1998 after a low of 63% in May 1972.[9] The fact is that we're not getting any worse, but we're not getting a whole lot better either.

So how do we generate more trust in our local government and begin to address the reasons why some people feel disengaged? To answer this, we need to understand how trust is created in local governance. Trust is produced when we demonstrate to citizens both our competence and trustworthiness. Trust lies at the intersection of both of these qualities. Herein lies one of the most persuasive arguments in favor of a community-based strategic planning endeavor; for when we engage in such an exercise and then show our resolve and capability

---

[8] Gallup poll, September 6–10, 2017, random sample of 1018 adults, age 18 and older.

[9] Gallup poll, September 7–11, 2016, random sample of 1017 adults, aged 18 and older.

to follow through with the plan, we demonstrate **both** competence and trustworthiness.

While we began to address the agitated citizenry factor as a possible obstacle to strategic planning, we are fully aware that many of you reading this may be enjoying relative calm in your community. We certainly hope so. For those of you who are, a strategic planning exercise will become one of the most beneficial things you can possibly do. An atmosphere of trust and cooperation provides the most fertile ground for a community-based strategic planning exercise. It will draw your staff, elected officials, and citizens even closer—and provide a spawning ground for some of the best ideas your community has ever contemplated.

For those who live and work within a community that is prone to political chaos, backbiting, and perhaps a dash of dysfunctionality, there is no more important thing you can embark upon than a community-based strategic planning project. Do not allow current upheavals and discontent to dissuade you from the very exercise that will unite your citizens and your civic officials. Many believe that it is appropriate to address strategic planning after the current chaos subsides; perhaps after the next election, perhaps when so-and-so is no longer on the council, board, or commission, perhaps when Mrs. so-and-so moves out of the community, perhaps when we get a new manager, perhaps, perhaps, perhaps. Days turn into months, and months turn into years; and we will be very blunt here in saying that some communities are never going to get better until they do something to bring people together. In this sense, it really isn't an agitated citizenry that poses an obstacle to strategic planning. It is many times our *fear* of "kicking the hive" of what we perceive to be an already agitated citizenry that puts the kibosh on this type of endeavor. Of course you're going to receive criticism from those who are already up in arms or who for any other reason don't think this is the time to plan your future. But you will witness how this type of exercise powerfully helps to silence the naysayers, restore purpose, and bring vision to your community.

Organizational Resistance

For many elected officials and public administrators, the internal situation at your local government may surface as a reason to delay or even avoid a strategic planning exercise. Similar to community turmoil, internal strife and low morale may convince us that this just isn't the time for such an endeavor and that it is probably best to wait until things subside.

It seems that for much of my career I have followed managers who took a much less open and definitely more traditional approach to management. One of my predecessors actually prohibited employees from approaching his doorway. If they needed to deliver a message to him, it was to be relayed through his administrative assistant. When I came to this organization, morale was at an all-time low. It was so bad that, a few weeks before my coming, the employee association actually encouraged members to show up at council meeting dressed in black in order to protest a recent change in health benefit administration. After my first four weeks on the job, my conversations and observations were enough to conclude that morale was not only a problem—it was the problem.

I put together a short survey of our employees to help me better understand and identify the causes of low morale. What came back was extraordinary. Employees indicated that a lack of communication and general disengagement were primary causes of low morale. Through a series of workshops that I presented with employees, we were able to identify more than 350 ideas to improve our workplace environment. More than 25% of these ideas specifically touched on enhancing communication between management and employees as well as re-engaging employees in problem solving. Actually, this survey served as the genesis for a handful of programs and initiatives designed to re-establish direct communication with employees and involve them in developing solutions. While bad morale dies very slowly, our consistent and persistent efforts to break down the communication barriers between management and employees as well as

involve our employees in constructive dialogue and problem-solving paid off big. When I left that city, morale had scarcely been higher.

We provide this example because the principles employed with local government staff are much the same as those employed in community strategic planning. Similar to an agitated citizenry, employee disengagement is often a product of staff that do not feel any real ownership in their organization. Many of these public servants feel like their duty is to "simply do what the boss says, keep your nose clean, and wait out the time until retirement." If an employee feels this way, exactly how productive do you imagine he or she is? How well served do you believe your citizens are? The reality is that employees will rarely treat your citizens better than they themselves are being treated. Unhappy municipal employees almost always result in unhappy citizens.

As mentioned previously, turning the morale of your organization around and re-engaging your employees is much like turning a cruise ship around in the ocean. It takes many turns of the wheel to make the least change in your course. It takes patience, consistency, and persistence. One of the reasons for this is because people are generally slow to believe the sincerity and survivability of any new management direction. Many of your employees, perhaps some of the more tenured, are even apt to say, "We tried this X number of years ago. It didn't work then, and it won't work now." The "been there done that" obstacle is one that you can expect as you introduce a strategic planning initiative in your community. Meanwhile, the likelihood that these folks have actually "been there and done that" or in other words have been involved in a bona fide community-based strategic planning exercise is usually remote. This is just their way of maintaining the status quo, which has served them well enough for many years. Likewise, others may oppose strategic planning simply because they don't trust the manager, the elected officials, and the citizens.

One suggestion for overcoming a trust deficit among your employees is to assure them that as an important stakeholder group in your community, they will definitely be invited to participate in the strategic planning process. Tell them that this exercise will represent a tremendous opportunity for them to provide feedback and direction in a very powerful way. As the process proceeds, you may also consider regularly updating employees about strategic planning progress. Since they are ultimately the implementers of citizen directives, they are likely to be very interested in seeing how these directives evolve through the course of the planning process.

For those institutional, status quo employees, it may be that many of them will not support the strategic planning process until they begin to see the fruits of that endeavor. It's possible that some of them will *never* support it. In these cases, you may once again need to take a page from Abraham Lincoln's playbook. On the question of what he would do with the Mormons in the newly organized State of Deseret (current day Utah, Nevada, Arizona, and most of Southern California), Lincoln told Mormon representative Thomas Stenhouse in 1863, "Stenhouse, when I was a boy on the farm . . . , there was a great deal of timber on the farm which we had to clear away. Occasionally, we would come to a log which had fallen down. It was too hard to split, too wet to burn, and too heavy to move, so we plowed around it. That's what I intend to do with the Mormons."[10]

As hard as it may be to come to grips with this reality, you're probably not going to get all employees to enthusiastically support a community-based strategic planning endeavor. The advice from Abraham Lincoln could apply to you. You're going to have to start the process so that they can witness the benefits for themselves. You may even win over a few converts along the way. We are not suggesting that you begin a process to which there is stiff internal opposition from the majority of local government employees. In our experience, this level of internal opposition is uncommon. It is much more likely that you will encounter

---

[10] Leonard J. Arrington and Davis Bitton, *The Mormon Experience: A History of the Latter-day Saints* (New York: Knopf, 1979).

a very small number who are less than enthusiastic about reaching out to the community as a means of assembling a strategic plan. Don't let a few get in the way of doing the right thing.

But what about getting the majority of employees on board with strategic planning? As discussed, many employees who would describe their internal atmosphere as less than optimal would likely agree that a lack of inclusion and appreciation are the primary causes of this organizational inversion. What better way to address both of these factors than through the involvement of employees in the strategic planning project? However, how you introduce strategic planning is even more critical than the project itself.

Our advice is to seek your employees' opinions from the beginning. Take some time before initiating the process to consult with them. These meetings will provide you with an opportunity to not only present strategic planning as an idea, but also help them understand the process and their specific role in creating the plan. You may also pick up some ideas from them that can truly benefit you and the community during the process. In so doing, you will begin your strategic planning endeavor by instilling real ownership on the part of employees. In addition, because of this sense of ownership, your employees will likely be more driven to support and implement the ideas that emerge from the plan.

Misperceptions

Within the walls of a typical municipal office, you will find stacked and stored, bound and shelved, an almost endless array of plans and special reports. Our experience is that many of these plans and reports have never been put into action in any meaningful way. It's true that those of us in municipal management many times feel like we are doing something about a problem if we study it and offer up a few recommendations. We may believe that the problem is so specialized and exotic that it requires the involvement of a consultant.

This may explain why a lot of opposition to strategic planning may be rooted in the fear that the local government is going to spend a lot of money for just another plan that's going to sit on the shelf and collect dust. Their fears are well-rooted. As described earlier, some communities have done exactly that. They've gone to great lengths to convince the administration and elected body that they need a plan, only to spend a lot of money composing it before they place it on a shelf where no one will ever read it again. If people do not understand and accept the unique approach and power associated with community-based strategic planning, you are likely to see their eyes glaze over when you surface the subject. The first task is therefore to explain the difference between a strategic planning endeavor and those efforts spent on composing other plans and reports. What are the differences?

> » *Community-based strategic planning is not internally driven nor created. It is a citizens' plan that articulates their expectations for local government.*

> » *Community-based strategic planning provides elected officials with a foundational blueprint for community goals and initiatives.*

> » *Community-based strategic planning provides the basis, therefore, upon which budgetary decisions will be made.*

> » *Community-based strategic planning represents a means of collecting the best ideas and most constructive feedback from the citizenry.*

In a nutshell, community-based strategic planning is different because it comes from the people who are being served. That is likely different from most every plan, study, or report your municipality has ever commissioned.

Next, some inside and outside of your organization may confuse a strategic plan with other municipal mainstays such as general plans and master plans. **I was recently asked by one elected official what the difference was between the general plan and a strategic plan. I explained to him that while a general plan provides the foundation upon which land use decisions and policies are based, a strategic plan** is a citizen vision for a community which articulates specific strategic directives and provides a blueprint for realizing those priorities. Another official declared proudly to me that their community was already on top of strategic planning. "We have a complete list of every capital project we're going to do within the next 20 years," he said, "and we have up-to-date master plans for sewer, water, and storm water."

While planning for the maintenance, repair, and expansion of critical infrastructure is important and even strategic, I had to tell this gentleman that such did not constitute a community-based strategic plan. This official, as I suppose many in municipal government do, suffered from a variety of misconceptions about strategic planning. These many times serve as the basis for opposing such a project. The table below summarizes these misconceptions and provides clarifications that can be used to help people better understand community-based strategic planning.

Misperception	Clarification
Strategic planning is expensive.	Because community-based strategic planning is citizen-driven, the costs are generally a fraction of other internal and consultant-driven studies. Typically, a citizens group called the Strategic Planning Advisory Committee (SPAC), often with the help and guidance of a consultant, plans information gathering activities, facilitates many of these events, and ultimately composes and presents the plan to the elected body.

Misperception	Clarification
We already have a strategic plan.	There are many different kinds of plans that masquerade as strategic plans. A capital improvement plan is not a strategic plan and a general plan is not a strategic plan. If you encounter this argument, try to understand clearly what plan they're referring to, and then respectfully explain the differences between that plan and a community-based strategic plan.
Community-based strategic planning will not succeed here because our citizens are not involved.	Strategic planning, in a community-based sense, is not about citizens coming to you. It's about you going to them. This is especially true if your citizens are not used to your asking for their opinion. The activities associated with strategic planning will involve tremendous outreach to various stakeholder groups and neighborhoods. Citizens generally desire to become re-engaged with their local government and will participate in the planning process if local government is willing to extend an invitation and demonstrate its earnestness.

Misperception	Clarification
We really do have a strategic plan, and it has never been used. Therefore, just doing another one is a waste of time and money.	Like our Alaskan community example earlier in the book, your community may have a strategic plan. However, did it involve the input of those being served? Likely, similar to our previous example, a group of very qualified and well-intentioned individuals composed that strategic plan. Remember one very important principle: ***The base of participation in composing your plan will determine its survivability and likelihood of implementation.***

CONCLUSION

There are any number of obstacles that you may confront as you begin laying the foundation for a community-based strategic planning project. These obstacles are most often the product of fear and misunderstanding. There is no possibility that this nor any other book can adequately anticipate all the roadblocks that people may throw in front of you. Naïve as it may seem, we hope that you encounter little to no opposition. Nevertheless, if you do, the key is to first thoroughly understand the opposition to strategic planning, whether such comes from citizens, elected officials, or even local government employees. Second, use these obstacles as opportunities to educate people about what community-based strategic planning is and what benefits it is likely to bring to your community and municipal organization. Third, make sure that elected and organizational leadership support the strategic planning initiative. Take the time to allow people to both intellectually and emotionally understand the concepts associated with the initiative. Remember to maintain respect and professionalism in all of your communications and interactions. The principles associated with strategic planning are the antithesis of the tactics of force and coercion. Move at a pace that allows people to follow, even when they have the choice not to.

TAKEAWAYS

» *Strategic planning is a leadership-supported and citizen-driven initiative. There is little to be gained from the exercise unless political and organizational leaders support the process and then have the will to do whatever it takes to make policy and allocate resources in alignment with the plan.*

» *Communities that wish to implement a strategic planning initiative will likely find obstacles in their paths. Opposition to strategic planning is usually caused by one or more of the following:*

  » *A lack of elected official and/or administrative support*

  » *An agitated citizenry*

  » *Organizational resistance*

  » *Misperceptions about strategic planning*

» *If your community is not accustomed to asking for public input, the idea of basing your strategic plan on citizen priorities is likely to make some people inside of your local government pretty nervous. You have the best chance at overcoming a trust deficit among your employees if you assure them that as a key stakeholder group in your community, they will be an important part of the strategic planning process.*

» *When your citizens speak as a larger voice, you will be surprised at how reasonable, logical, and constructive the feedback is. Regardless of what appears feasible or infeasible, an articulated community priority provides your municipal government with the opportunity to acquaint citizens with the process of planning for such an amenity, facility, or program.*

» *Community-based strategic planning is ultimately a tool to help elected policymakers do their job with more confidence, clarity, and political will. Staff needs to understand that the byproduct of this process is likely to be facilitated goal-setting and a smoother budget process.*

» *Trust is produced when we demonstrate to citizens both our competence and trustworthiness. Trust lies at the intersection of both of these qualities. Herein lies perhaps one of the most persuasive arguments in favor of a community-based strategic planning endeavor. When we engage in such an exercise, and then show our resolve and capability to follow through with the plan, we demonstrate both critical ingredients that lead to greater trust.*

3

LAYING OUT THE PROCESS

———

"The future belongs to those who believe in the beauty of their dreams."
— Eleanor Roosevelt

When I was quite young, I noticed one day that my father had acquired quite a number of cologne and aftershave bottles, each only partially filled. With that desire to be helpful typical of a six-year-old, I proceeded to consolidate all of my dad's aftershaves and colognes into a smaller number of bottles. It seemed like a very sensible thing to do, given that it would create much more space in my father's rather small medicine cabinet. However, I did not consider that the random mixture of so many fragrances would create such a stench! It's not that my intention was bad. I had simply given very little thought to how all the elements would ultimately work together.

Like the cologne experiment, many people who would otherwise be champions of inclusion and strategic planning have been dissuaded because of their past experiences with the public in general and committees specifically. There's an old saying sometimes resonating in their heads that "a camel is a horse that was created by committee." They have found through unfortunate circumstance that unilateral planning and action is preferable to the nuisance associated with trying to get everyone together on the same page. What they miss, however, is that their inclination to include people in decision-making and planning is not wrong. Most often, their process just needs some work.

Again, like the cologne and aftershave consolidation, those planning to engage in a strategic planning process need to be careful to design that process in a way that maximizes the experiences, the insights, and the collective wisdom of those participating in such a way that optimizes the outcome (the strategic plan and its successful execution). Randomly throwing people together and directing them to come up with a vision for your community is no more a successful process than mixing random fragrances. You're likely to create something that stinks. Therefore, every bit of energy and time you spend up front in laying out the process of your strategic plan initiative will return dividends in the form of clearer citizen input, greater cooperation, and broader citizen acceptance of the plan.

In this chapter, we explain the first phases of the strategic planning process. In the interest of avoiding redundancy, we begin with the assumption that you have broad acceptance among your community's leadership infrastructure. That means that your elected officials are on board and that you have explained your intentions to senior staff. You also hopefully feel like the majority of your employees are on board too.

In this chapter, we focus on the importance of the strategic planning committee, its orientation and expectations, and the use of stakeholder groups and optional subcommittees. We will also address how you might be able to avoid some of the pitfalls occasionally associated with the initial stages of strategic planning.

The Strategic Planning Advisory Committee

Hopefully by this point you completely understand that the strategic planning process is leadership supported but remains a citizen initiative. Without your community's leadership firmly behind this endeavor, it will not succeed. Likewise, without citizen ownership of the process, the end product will not be legitimized or acknowledged. Both elements are absolutely critical to the success of community-based strategic planning.

We therefore begin strategic planning with the selection of citizen volunteers who will serve throughout the strategic planning process. These citizens will serve as the faces of strategic planning in your community. They will be the ambassadors and cheerleaders for strategic planning. They also become liaisons between the elected body and the citizens themselves. We affectionately refer to this group as the SPAC (Strategic Planning Advisory Committee).

The SPAC is most often composed of 7 to 9 individuals appointed by the elected body. We choose that many members generally because we expect to see one or two drop out somewhere along the process. It isn't that you selected the wrong people as much as it is that lives change, priorities change, and demands change. In no case do you want less than about five active members of your committee.

In order for this initiative to be successful, it is critically important that the elected body chooses citizens who have the qualities and abilities necessary for this type of endeavor. They need to be people of sound judgment, devoid of strong ideological motivations and agendas, and absolutely trustworthy. SPAC members should be well-educated with experience in business or public administration, people who have perhaps had experience with strategic planning at some time in their careers, whether functioning in the business world or in government. Members should not be selected based on their popularity in the community, their tenure as a resident, their status as a former elected official or candidate, or any other reasons unrelated to the tasks at hand. Because they will be guiding this process, inviting public participation, reporting progress, composing the plan, and presenting it for ratification, SPAC members need to be individuals of unquestionable integrity and competency. While it is not necessary to select SPAC members in a way that ensures exactly equal representation from all quarters of your community, it does help to have a good cross section of your community reflected in the SPAC because the SPAC members will be a key element of the community outreach. Tapping into their ties to different sectors of the community will be very valuable in conducting that outreach.

Selecting who should be a member of the strategic planning committee is certainly one thing. Extending the invitation, explaining the expectations, and getting them to commit is quite another. Before you begin contact with potential committee members, it would be a good idea to have a few additional names in your back pocket just in case those to whom you initially extend invitations decline. While it's best that the elected body develop a list of potential committee members, the mayor should personally and individually extend an invitation to participate on the strategic planning committee. As he or she does so, it's best to set the stage by leading off with an explanation of why your community feels so strongly about pursuing this initiative. The mayor should also explain to the SPAC candidate the important role that he or she will have on the committee and why the elected body felt strongly about including him or her. Finally, it's appropriate to also explain what will be expected of each committee member and what the community hopes to do or achieve with this new plan.

Just what will be expected? You can begin by telling them that they will likely be required to meet as a committee over the next 6 to 8 months, as little as twice a month initially and weekly as the process draws closer to conclusion. Tell them that they will need to bring their best ideas and judgment; that they will be asked to take what they learn from citizens and synthesize it into a roadmap for their community. Helping them understand that there is an end date to the service can be critical in getting otherwise busy people to commit. If it feels like an open-ended commitment, recruitment for the SPAC becomes more difficult.

There may be several questions or concerns expressed by the committee candidate when the invitation is extended. Some of these have already been articulated earlier in this book. He or she may simply feel like their life is too complicated and full to enable them to completely commit. They may have had a bad experience serving on a committee in the past. They may even doubt the sincerity of the municipal government with regard to implementing the plan once it's created. Whatever the roadblock, make sure that you do not press anyone into service. It is essential that each member of the committee *desires* to be there, unobligated by a guilt trip.

Once your elected body has invited citizens to participate as part of the SPAC and they have accepted the assignment, the elected body should by resolution establish a strategic planning advisory committee and officially ratify the names appointed to this committee. It's also important to name and appoint a committee chair, someone who you believe can provide the steady leadership necessary to sustain this planning endeavor. It should be someone that other committee members will respect and who epitomizes the ideal committee member—i.e. professional, devoid of ideological ambition, not politically motivated, etc. This is the person who will be running your SPAC meetings and speaking for the group before the elected body and citizen groups. It therefore behooves you to be extremely careful about who to tap for this important responsibility. In addition, it is wise to assign a staff person to be a liaison to the committee. Generally, a senior administrative person would be most appropriate. The staff person can serve as a general help to the committee, facilitating access to information and resources.

Public ratification or announcement of the committee and its members provides a wonderful opportunity for elected officials to launch the strategic planning initiative, articulate once again why they feel strongly about this endeavor, and generally educate the public about the process and expected outcomes. It's appropriate to invite not only the committee members but also their family members to be in attendance. In every regard, you want to make sure that your committee members feel from the very beginning the importance of their responsibilities. You may ask at this point, speaking of "committee," why I would not recommend that you establish a commission instead of just a committee. This really depends on your own preference and maybe even the laws associated with your specific jurisdiction. I tend to lean in the direction of establishing a committee for a couple of reasons.

First, depending on your state's open meeting laws, commissions may be subject to certain requirements that do not apply to committees. For example, in many states, as long as a committee does not make final decisions, but merely makes recommendations to the governing body, it may not be subject to open meeting laws. Therefore, based on the work that strategic planning committees perform, it is likely that the SPAC would be exempted from those requirements. Contrastingly, in some states, as long as the elected body appoints those serving, regardless of whether you call them a committee or commission, they are subject to open meeting laws. In such cases, it may be necessary to appoint the SPAC as a subcommittee of a larger committee or commission. The bottom line is that it's best to check your individual state law before establishing a committee or a commission.

It's not necessary that the committee work in secrecy, but you don't want to burden them with a wheelbarrow full of extra requirements either. To be effective, the SPAC needs to be a collaborative group, not a stuffy policy-setting body. If every one of their meetings is a public and open meeting, you're likely to have someone in your community who feels like they've got to "keep an eye" on the committee's work and otherwise exert influence on the process. This is not likely to be productive.

The second reason we lean in the direction of a strategic planning committee is that commissions themselves usually have quasi-judicial and even some legislative powers bequeathed to them by the elected body. Our experience is that many of them tend to, over the course of their existence, take on a life of their own, especially if they do not begin their existence with a full understanding and recognition of their scope of responsibilities. We have noticed over time that individuals who function on a committee usually have an easier time understanding their subordinate role to the body that created them—the elected body in the case of strategic planning. We have witnessed how some commissions "grow up" to eventually *eat* their owner. Allow us to provide an example.

During my management tenure in Arizona, the elected body there decided to create an official commission for strategic planning that would remain engaged as a body not only throughout the strategic planning process, but during the months and years of implementation as well. As we will discuss further in the book, municipal strategic plans are best laid out in five year increments. In my Arizona community, the strategic planning commission would continue to meet, monitor plan progress, and even provide additional advice to the elected body between years one and five. This would on the face appear to be a sensible arrangement, and we recommend in this book that your SPAC remain engaged beyond plan creation. However, without an entirely clear understanding or acceptance of their charter, the commission began to issue orders to staff and began to formulate priorities and initiatives not originally part of the strategic plan. The way commission members saw it, the strategic plan was a living and breathing organism that could be modified at any time by the commission.

To some degree, plan directives did become somewhat organic, and this made implementation tricky to say the least. For example, a few years into plan implementation, the strategic planning advisory commission determined that the elected body was not focused enough on the fiscal sustainability of the community. Since the municipality lacked a primary property tax, the commission began to advocate for a community property tax as a means of diversifying the community's coffers. Advocacy turned into demands. In fact, the commission revisited the strategic plan and edited parts of it to include a primary local property tax as a strategic initiative. They also sent letters advocating the property tax to both the elected body and the media.

Fortunately, most of the elected officials saw what was evolving early on and were able to minimize the political tension between the two groups. And it's not just about strategic planning commissions. We've also seen planning commissions and other internal groups take on a life and spirit of their own that eventually clashed with the elected body. These two reasons adequately summarize why we favor establishing a strategic planning advisory *committee*, not commission, making sure that members understand what their role is in creating the plan and their limited role in reporting plan progress later. Meanwhile, we strongly believe that the elected body and administration themselves represent the best means of both implementing plan elements and monitoring progress toward plan realization. While the SPAC can assist with plan monitoring and reporting, the primary responsibility for execution and follow through should remain with administration and elected officials.

SPAC Orientation and Launch

If you have ever had the opportunity to serve on a committee, you recognize the interesting dynamics associated with bringing a group together of differing backgrounds, expertise, skill sets, perspectives, and personalities. While this book is not about group dynamics or how to run an effective committee meeting, we will go so far as to say that the most critical thing you can do at your first SPAC meeting is to allow members to become acquainted with each other and present them with the opportunity to begin appreciating what each brings in terms of expertise, perspective, etc. This can be done in a variety of ways.

Strategic planning meetings can be facilitated by either the chair or a professional facilitator. Generally speaking, it's best that the SPAC maintain its independence from elected officials and staff, so I wouldn't recommend an elected or chief appointed official as the facilitator. If the chair doesn't feel entirely comfortable about facilitating every meeting—and there could be a number of reasons for this including a lack of familiarity with the process—our recommendation is that you utilize a professional facilitator or strategic planning consultant.

Regardless, at the first orientation and meeting, you will want to start with an icebreaker that requires each committee member to tell the group a little something about their background and then perhaps one thing about themselves that they believe nobody else would know. Sharing information like this about oneself creates vulnerability, a powerful and important ingredient that builds trust. Renowned researcher and Ted Talker Dr. Brené Brown says this about the power of vulnerability: "Vulnerability is the birthplace of connection and the path to the feeling of worthiness. If it doesn't feel vulnerable the sharing is probably not constructive."[11]

And don't stop with this exercise. Anything you can do to introduce your committee members to each other and help them to appropriately increase their vulnerability is a wise investment of time. You have all been in your first committee meeting before, your first study group, your first whatever group. This can seem like a scene out of a Clint Eastwood movie where it feels like each person is waiting for the other to draw his or her weapon. A lot of things go through your mind when you first meet people, and seldom are any of them fair, true, or real. If our thoughts could be heard they would probably be embarrassing, insulting, and terribly entertaining. "That guy's trying to hide the fact that he's bald with that comb-over technique. That's all we need on this committee, some guy who can't come to grips with the fact that he's turning into Kojak." "That's a real nice look, lady. Sweatpants in public."

We have learned over the years, and this is backed up by a lot of research, that as a defense mechanism, we tend to be harsh on people we don't know. We look for the weaknesses in others as a way to assuage our own feelings of inadequacy. After all, if somebody throws us into a committee, we want to feel at least equal to the other members and preferably superior. Your first order of business therefore with your new

---

[11] Brené Brown, *The Power of Vulnerability: Teachings on Authenticity, Connection, and Courage* (Sounds True, 2012). Audiobook.

strategic planning committee is to assist committee members in taking off their emotional armor and becoming human to each other. Why? Because when our defenses are up, our best ideas remain inside. We are less apt to share because the last thing we want is our ideas mocked, minimized, or dismissed. Dr. Brown sums it up this way, "Vulnerability is about showing up and being seen. It's tough to do that when we're terrified about what people might see or think."[12]

Another important reason we want to increase vulnerability and generally get to know the real us is that committee dissent and distrust usually have their genesis in the first couple of meetings. I already mentioned our tendency to draw false conclusions about others. As we do so, we start to notice and even exaggerate the characteristics of others that enable us to justify the way we feel about them. There is a groundbreaking book produced by the Arbinger Institute called *The Anatomy of Peace* that describes this self-justification as "being in the box." They describe this condition as follows: "Whenever we need to be justified, anything that will give us justification will immediately take on exaggerated importance in our life."[13]

This is one of the most powerful explanations of why some committees never seem to gel. It had nothing to do with the competency of its individual members or their worthiness to serve on the committee. It's just that they came with their emotional armor and no one ever told them that they needed to leave it at home. As time progressed, the differences and even weaknesses that each member brought to meetings not only became exaggerated, but served as fuel for greater dissension and disagreement. For this reason, don't be in a big hurry to get to business until you pay attention to the important task of relationship

---

[12] Brown, *The Power of Vulnerability.*

[13] Arbinger Institute, *The Anatomy of Peace: Resolving the Heart of Conflict* (San Francisco: Berrett-Koehler, 2006), 106.

building. Once you believe you are on firm emotional footing, you can take the next step, which entails mapping the strategic planning process.

Mapping the Process

The legendary Yogi Berra liked to say, "If you don't know where you are going, you might wind up someplace else."[14] This is definitely true when it comes to the strategic planning process. That is why it is extremely important to not only begin your community-based strategic planning endeavor by building relationships among your committee members, but by also completely understanding as a committee how this process is going to roll out. Generally, your process map is going to include four elements:

» *The Mission Statement*
» *The Outline*
» *The Timeline*
» *The Budget*

The Mission Statement

The first thing that we recommend to a strategic planning committee is to establish a mission statement that captures the very essence of why your committee exists and what it has been tasked to accomplish. This exercise helps committee members get on the same page. In the absence of such a mutual understanding, it is very common for committee members to, as we describe often with regard to elected officials, "get into the weeds." Perhaps an example may help explain.

We were assisting a very beautiful yet less-than-developed community with their strategic plan. It was during one of our committee meetings that a member of our SPAC proposed a new direction for the strategic plan. He proposed to the group an exercise whereby citizens would be invited to help plan the future development of the community. In his

---

[14] Yogi Berra Quotes. n.d. BrainyQuote.com. Accessed February 8, 2015, www.brainyquote.com/quotes/yogi_berra_391900.

description, groups of individuals would gather around large tables and physically place objects on a large map of the area. Each object would be labeled as a future amenity, business, or institution that citizens envisioned coming to their community. At the end of the exercise, this gentleman suggested that the SPAC then consolidate the exercises from the various tables into a unified vision of their community.

All of the committee members just seemed to sit in silence with their eyes fixated on the area of the table immediately in front of their faces. **I piped up first and mentioned that I had actually been through a similar exercise in the first community where I was a municipal manager. I mentioned that the exercise was very helpful in allowing us to visually construct what we believed our future should be. The exercise assisted us in making changes to our general land use plan. In my mind I knew that this was an exercise more appropriate for land-use planning, not strategic planning. I was beating around the bushes, trying not to offend the committee member who had just left the pathway of our project and was now neck-deep "in the weeds." That's when my partner, Dan Griffiths, less apt to beat around the bushes, stated to the group "That's a very interesting idea, but one that's probably more appropriate for a planning commission than for our strategic planning committee." He then went on to remind the committee of their central mission, and the focus returned for the SPAC.** It's not that the exercise being proposed by the committee member was not intriguing and engaging. The problem was that this exercise would have taken the committee in a different direction and convoluted what they were trying to accomplish. Please understand here that we're not suggesting to you that the exercise suggested by our committee member is not or would not be appropriate for your specific strategic planning endeavor. That's the point here. The reality is that it was *not* in alignment with what *this* particular SPAC's charter was. In this case, the strategic planning committee was tasked with identifying the most important community priorities and then prescribing initiatives that would allow their community to deliver on those priorities.

Your particular mission statement should likewise capture the very essence of what you've been asked to accomplish, and it should be done in just a sentence or two. As an example, it may look something like this:

> **"Our mission as a strategic planning advisory committee is to invite citizens, businesses, and other stakeholders to craft our mutual expectations, dreams, and hopes for our community and to articulate this shared vision in a community strategic plan."**

Here we have communicated three key activities for the strategic planning committee: inviting participation, crafting expectations/dreams/hopes, and articulating a vision. We also describe who will be involved in these activities: citizens, businesses, and other stakeholders. In essence, your strategic planning mission should answer three questions: Who? What? How?

WHO   Citizens, businesses, and other stakeholders
WHAT   Craft our mutual expectations, dreams, and hopes for our community
HOW   Inviting, crafting, and articulating

Once you have completed your mission statement, make sure that somebody, preferably with legible handwriting, writes this statement on a large sticky note for display at every one of your meetings. It will not only keep you on track, but it will also be a powerful reminder of the important nature of your work.

The Outline

Many of you will probably remember completing outlines for book reports, research papers, and other assignments in school. It serves as a "to do" list. In an outline, we detail tasks and milestones that need to be completed if we are to fulfill our mission. These tasks and milestones are placed in a chronological order. In the context of strategic planning, your outline will detail the four primary phases of strategic planning: launch, data gathering, analysis, and composition. Much of your understanding specific to each one of these phases will come from your complete reading of this book. So be patient if you don't completely understand a few of the terms used in the outline below. It's also natural for a few questions to surface as you're reading through this outline. Be assured that we will endeavor to answer each.

Under the individual sections corresponding with the four phases, you will list the tasks assigned to each section and the activities associated with those tasks. Here's an example of a strategic planning outline.

Strategic Planning Outline

"Our mission as a strategic planning advisory committee is to invite citizens, businesses, and other stakeholders to craft our mutual expectations, dreams, and hopes for our community and to articulate this shared vision in a community strategic plan."

I.   *Launch*
   A   *Prescribe data-gathering activities, dates, and times*
   B   *Determine format for public meetings*
   C   *Develop data-gathering instruments*
   D   *Identify communication channels through which citizens, businesses, and stakeholders may be invited to participate in data-gathering exercises*
   E   *Identify all stakeholder groups*
   F   *Develop and execute a branding and communications strategy to encourage participation*

II. *Data Gathering*
   A   *Work with staff or a consultant to develop and administer an online citizen survey*

    B   *Schedule and execute focus groups with identified stakeholders*

    C   *Schedule and hold public open houses*

    D   *Work with the chamber to hold strategic planning workshops with businesses*

    E   *Work with the school district to hold focus groups with parent/teacher organizations*

    F   *Create a central data repository*

III. *Analysis*

    A   *Gather all results/responses*

    B   *Begin synthesizing results into broad subject areas*

    C   *Begin identifying strategic directives*

IV. *Composition*

    A   *Fully develop strategic directives*

    B   *Develop strategic initiatives associated with each directive*

    C   *Identify all toolbox items*

    D   *Completely develop composition of strategic plan and format for presentation*

    E   *Present plan to elected body for formal adoption*

Phases of the Strategic Planning Process

Phase	Explanation	Possible Activities
Launch	The Launch Phase of the strategic planning process represents a time during which the formats for public data-gathering activities and events are constructed. It is also a time when the local government's intention to pursue a strategic plan is generally communicated to citizens. It's a time to identify critical stakeholder groups and schedule data-gathering events.	» Determine number and type of data-gathering activities. » Make public announcement of a strategic planning initiative. » Identify critical stakeholder groups. » Schedule public meetings. » Design online data-gathering. » Create strategic planning calendar.
Data Gathering	As the name denotes, this is a time when public events and activities are executed. This represents the largest period of time in the process.	» Hold public meetings. » Administer online survey. » Hold focus group meetings.
Analysis	The Analysis Phase represents the time when the strategic planning committee begins to interpret data collected in the previous phase. It is a time when we see the earliest development of the plan directives.	» Synthesize data into strategic directives (broad statements of community priorities).

Phases of the Strategic Planning Process		
Composition	Composition is when directives are refined and strategic initiatives (the milestones of the plan) are created. It is also during this time that more specific toolbox items are identified and tied to relevant strategic directives. In short, the Composition Phase is when the committee determines and articulates all elements associated with the strategic plan. It is during this phase also that the committee determines the format of the final plan.	» Finalize strategic directives. » Compose strategic initiatives. » Identify and categorize toolbox elements by strategic directive. » Determine final format of plan. » Determine timing of public presentation.

THE TIMELINE

One of the most common questions we receive is "How long is all of this going to take?" It is a natural question. Most elected officials want to make sure they are still in office when the plan is completed. The answer is (and we know of no one who likes to hear this): "It depends." There are many questions that would need to be answered before the determination of the timeline can be made. Certainly, the strategic planning committee is in the best position of determining a timeline. However, allow us to share a few principles that may guide your determination.

We have already discussed how the broadening of participation in your plan correlates with its survivability. Furthermore, the broader your participation in creating the plan, the more data you are able to collect, and the clearer your strategic directives will become. It's like the pixels in a television or computer monitor. The more pixels you have, the clearer the picture. Likewise, the more citizens that participate in providing their feedback and input, the clearer and more determinable are the community priorities that your plan will communicate. Therefore, if you want to begin and complete a strategic planning exercise in a month or two, it is appropriate to accept the corresponding risk that your plan may not entirely represent all elements or priorities of your community. As a general rule, the larger the population, the more time it takes to gather data, make sense of it, and compose the plan. Likewise, the more diverse your community is, the more time you're going to want to take to make sure that all stakeholders have had a chance to chime in. As a general rule, we do not recommend a process less than 4 to 6 months. Most of the time, for communities less than 50,000 residents, the entire process runs 6 to 8 months. For those communities of over 100,000, you can expect your process to take as much as a year. Keep in mind that there are no hard and fast rules about how long your process should be. It does indeed depend on the amount of inclusion either desired or required to lend validity to the outcomes.

So why does it take so long? Looking at the phases that we outlined on the previous page, there is really only one that requires more than a few weeks to a month to complete. The Data Gathering Phase will consume 60% or more of the total time allotted to the strategic planning process. Data-gathering activities need to be calendared, scheduled, and held in times and places that maximize participation. You also need to give ample time for your citizens to utilize online methods of providing feedback. You may also want your data-gathering activities to coincide with certain events and activities where you believe a considerable number of citizens will be gathered. All of this requires time.

The key to success in strategic planning is this important principle: *Maximize opportunities to participate and don't rush it.* Remember that slow is smooth and smooth is fast. The last thing that you want to have happen is the accusation that you were only interested in the opinions of a few. One of the key pieces of information you are going to want to share at the conclusion of your process is how many people actually took the time to provide their opinions and general feedback. If you have enjoyed broad participation, this will legitimize your process and increase your plan's survivability.

There is of course such a thing as too much of anything. You certainly don't want to stall your plan in the Data Gathering Phase, determined to interview every single citizen in your community. Make sure that you pre-scribe ample but *finite* time for data gathering. As a base of consideration and a beginning point of determining your timeline, use the chart on the following page.

Estimated Time Frames Per Phase				
	Six Months	Eight Months	Ten Months	Twelve Months
Launch	2 weeks	3 weeks	4 weeks	5 weeks
Data Gathering	15 weeks	19 weeks	23 weeks	30 weeks
Analysis	4 weeks	6 weeks	8 weeks	10 weeks
Composition	3 weeks	4 weeks	5 weeks	7 weeks

You may elect to use a Gantt chart to lay out the process. A Gantt chart is a type of bar chart that illustrates a project schedule. It shows the start and finish dates of key elements of a project, allows you to break down the structure of the project, and importantly illustrates the dependency relationships between activities.

On the following page is what your strategic planning process could look like portrayed in a Gantt chart. It's also important to consider the timing of your launch. For example, in most communities in the United States, January and September tend to be ideal launch times. This is because trying to do data gathering during the summer or between

Thanksgiving and New Year's tends to result in diminished citizen participation. Prime time for data gathering is typically mid-January through May and then again in mid-September through mid-November.

STRATEGIC PLANNING PROCESS

This is obviously a very simplified Gantt chart. The flexibility of the Gantt allows you to place as much detail as you would like into each phase. We recommend maintaining simplicity.

	Jan	Feb	Mar	Apr	May	Jun	Jul	Aug
Launch	▓							
Data Gathering		▓	▓	▓	▓			
Analysis						▓	▓	▓
Composition							▓	▓

The purpose of the chart is to ensure that you are able to quickly appraise the progress of the project and make necessary adjustments to keep it on schedule. As this chart illustrates, there is nothing wrong with beginning your analysis before all of the data gathering is complete. Likewise, formatting the report and some composition can begin while you are still analyzing the data.

The Budget

Community-based strategic planning is not inherently an expensive process. If you choose to utilize a facilitator to help guide your process, as well as help analyze data and compose the report, such will represent your project's primary expense. Many communities choose to utilize a professional strategic planning facilitator for reasons which we have mentioned and will discuss later on in this book. The decision to utilize a facilitator, meanwhile, should be made by the elected body prior to the establishment of the strategic planning committee. Beyond that expense, you may encounter some minimal costs associated with public outreach. (We discuss this in the next chapter.) However, beyond these two, there really are very few expenses. Nevertheless, you are going to confront the need to provide some materials for workshops and focus groups. Additionally, there may be other nominal costs associated with gathering data and producing the report. It is therefore important that you spend a small amount of time in your committee determining all needed materials and supplies. Prior to beginning the project, it's also a good idea to sit down with your chief administrator to not only talk out the process, but also discuss some of the needs of the committee. You will probably find that he or she is more than happy to allow use of facilities and materials for this project. The local government is likely to allow the SPAC to use its newsletter, website, and email groups to invite citizen participation. It is also advisable that administration appoint a staff liaison that can help bring resources to bear during the process. Ideally, this will be someone other than the municipal manager. Often an assistant or someone with PR responsibilities can be a good choice.

CONCLUSION

Careful planning of your strategic planning process is critical to success. Since community-based strategic planning is a citizen initiative, the elected body should appoint citizens to oversee and direct the strategic planning process. These citizen volunteers will form part of the strategic planning advisory committee (SPAC). They need to be objective individuals of high integrity and experience. They also need to be devoid of political or ideological agendas and trusted in the community. It also helps if each member has had experience in his or her profession with the concepts of strategic planning. The first order of business is to spend time allowing your committee members to acquaint themselves with the strengths, perspectives, and unique character of each member. The time you spend early in the process to allow your committee to normalize and become comfortable with each other will pay dividends later as a group is called upon to unite in making difficult decisions. In order to minimize the chance that the process gets off track, the committee should articulate in writing a mission statement that defines the committee's charter and assignment. Additionally, the group can benefit from the exercise of formulating an outline which clearly articulates activities associated with each of the four phases of strategic planning: launch, data gathering, analysis, and composition. Applying or associating these steps with expected time frames is also important. In general, more than half of the strategic planning process will be assigned to data gathering. The final element of pre-planning entails determining what materials, supplies, and physical space will be needed by the committee. The primary costs will probably be related to the use of a professional facilitator, if so desired, and public outreach activities. It is important to capture all of these costs and present them to administration. Usually, the municipal government is more than happy to provide the committee with access to materials, supplies, equipment, facilities, and even citizen outreach media such as newsletters, websites, email groups, etc. They may even assign staff as liaisons to support the work of the committee.

TAKEAWAYS

» *Those planning to engage in a strategic planning process need to be careful to design that process in a way that maximizes the experiences, insights, and collective wisdom of those participating in such a way that optimizes the final plan.*

» *Every bit of energy and time you spend up front in laying out the process of your strategic planning initiative will return dividends in the form of clearer citizen input, greater cooperation, and broader citizen acceptance of the plan.*

» *Without your community's leadership being firmly behind this endeavor, it will not succeed. Likewise, without citizen ownership of the process, the end product will not be legitimized or acknowledged. Both elements are absolutely critical to the success of community-based strategic planning.*

» *Because this is a citizen-driven initiative, the elected body should begin the strategic planning process by appointing volunteer citizens to be part of the strategic planning advisory committee (SPAC). This group should be composed of individuals devoid of political agenda or extreme ideologies. They should be trusted individuals and preferably have some experience with the concepts associated with strategic planning.*

» *Don't neglect relationship and trust building among advisory committee members. The trust among committee members is a key factor in your ultimate success.*

» *The committee can maximize success by taking the time to carefully plan their process. A blueprint for the strategic planning process should include four elements: the mission, the outline, the time frame, and the budget.*

4

TIPS FOR WORKING WITH THE ELECTED BODY

———

"Nearly all men can stand adversity, but if you want to test
a man's character, give him power."
— *Abraham Lincoln*

If you've been around municipal government for any amount of time, you've probably observed a heated exchange during a meeting of the elected body. What never ceases to amaze us is the unpredictability of some of the emotional outbursts. Seemingly benign issues can spark a flurry of controversy while other much more substantive matters can sail right through as if they were approving the minutes.

In her book, "Presence," Harvard Business School professor Amy Cuddy describes how we initially assess people using two main criteria: warmth and competence.

1. *Can I trust this person?*

2. *Can I respect this person?*

Interestingly, your level of trustworthiness is the most important factor in how people perceive you.

When we feel threatened, these criteria take on even greater importance. Joseph Grenny, author of Crucial Conversations, describes how our brain fixates on two related questions.

1.   *Do you mean me harm?*

2.   *Do you have the capacity to carry it out?*

In moments of high stress, our brain tends to assume that the answer to the second question is "yes." In such moments, figuratively speaking, the person in front of us is carrying a gun on her hip. The only question our brain is trying to answer is, **do they intend to use it**.

When our brain answers both of these questions in the affirmative, a powerful biological response is triggered. To understand this response, we need to have a quick refresher on brain anatomy. Our primitive brain, the limbic system sits on top of our spinal column and beneath the gray matter we typically think of when we envision the brain. Our more advanced brain is the gray matter, the two hemispheres with all of the folds in them that sit on top, the neo cortex. This is where all rational thought occurs. This is where our capacity for language resides. This is where we make connections between different ideas. This is where logic lives.

Our more primitive brain has no such capacity and it is the place where emotion originates. It has no capacity for language or higher-order thinking. Many of the structures in this part of the brain are shared by other members of the animal kingdom like reptiles and birds. You will sometimes hear scientists refer to this part of the brain as our reptilian brain. When our brain concludes that we are under threat (they have a gun and they intend to use it), the primitive part of our brain seizes control. It does this by constricting the blood flow into our more advanced brain, our gray matter. This restricts our capacity for rational thought and puts us in a highly reactive "fight or flight" mode.

So, what does this have to do with the strategic planning process and how to work with your elected body? Serving as an elected official is a stressful experience. Sitting up on that dais can place our nervous system in a state of high alert where it appears that everyone in the room has a gun on their hip. Public office is hard on people. *I previously served on the Utah State Board of Education. I remember coming home from State School Board meetings in a state of complete exhaustion. As an elected official, I felt like I was in the line of fire.*

It's critical that you appreciate this dynamic as you approach the strategic planning process. Up until this point, the experience of most of your elected officials with public gatherings of citizens will have been largely negative. Town hall meetings with angry residents tend to make elected officials reluctant to want to ask residents what they think for fear of getting hit with some rotten tomatoes or worse.

RECOMMENDATION #1 – CREATE SAFETY

Take the time to meet one-on-one with each elected official to paint the picture for them. If you bring up community-based strategic planning during a public meeting and all you have done is to provide a heads up to the mayor, you're likely to make your elected officials think that you've got a gun and you intend to use it. Spend dedicated one-on-one time to address concerns in a safe setting and help them understand how this process is going to make their lives easier.

> **During a public meeting, I once observed an elected official take nearly 20 minutes to stand on a soap box and criticize his fellow council members in every way imaginable. He carried on so long that the mayor finally had to intervene. One week later, I observed this same elected official have a very civil discussion with fellow council members during a council work session with the same topic of discussion. Why the change in tone?**

Public meetings of elected officials and the layout of the rooms in which they are held are structured to project power. Elected officials typically sit on a dais raised above the floor. Each elected official has a fancy push-to-talk microphone and a shiny nameplate so that everyone can see how important they are. The "little people" approach the seat of power from a small table or podium that is beneath the elected officials on the dais. These meetings do not engender safety. Quite the contrary. They reinforce to the minds of everyone there the presence of a holstered gun on the hip of everyone in the room. It is very difficult to create enough safety in this environment to have open dialogue about a community-based strategic planning initiative.

During a work session, however, it is much more common for elected officials to be seated around a table, on the same level with everyone else in the room. This was the case with the work session that we described above. The same elected official that behaved as a raving ideologue hurling personal insults at his fellow council members was actually quite civil during the work session. The only thing that had changed was the layout of the room and consequently, the perceived safety on the part of all meeting participants.

If possible, it can really help to conduct any initial discussion about the planning process during a work session as opposed to a more formal meeting. You want to create enough safety to allow open dialogue and discussion among elected officials and avoid triggering the primitive reptilian part of their brain and the emotional, irrational response that follows. A one-on-one discussion with each elected official prior to this group discussion will also go a long way in keeping the reptilian brain in check.

RECOMMENDATION #2 – TAKE THE HEAT OFF

We've described how elected officials often feel like they are in the line of fire. Help them understand how a community-based planning process can take some of the heat off. Emphasize how the process will help to insulate the elected body from the rotten tomatoes that often get thrown around in public meetings. By appointing a strategic planning advisory committee, you are creating a buffer between citizens and elected officials. This takes some of the pressure off of the elected body and allows for much more open sharing, discussion, deliberation, and ultimately gives the elected body some cover as they make decisions that align with community priorities articulated in the plan that the advisory committee develops. Do you remember the story we shared in the first chapter about the spring training facility? That's the kind of picture you want to paint for your elected officials. This initiative will give you the power and political cover to say yes to those things that citizens have identified as most important and no to other good things that fall outside of those key priorities.

At a municipal retreat, I once listened to an elected official share the following. "Before I won my election, I felt like I had a very good relationship with my neighbors. Almost as soon as I took office, that relationship seemed to change. Suddenly, I was no longer a neighbor looking to serve the community. I had become one of those evil politicians."

This dynamic is very real in most communities. Residents can come to see elected officials as evil politicians and local government staff as evil bureaucrats. This is why the appointment of an independent group of volunteers to serve on the committee is such a critical element. Whatever you can do to demonstrate that this is truly a citizen-led process, largely independent of the influence of the evil politicians and bureaucrats, will significantly improve your odds of success.

Taking some of the heat off can be a huge selling point for your elected body. There are also biological reasons why this is important. The stress response that we described earlier is something that tends to do a very good job of keeping us from taking action. Fear paralyzes. Anger leads to aggression. Neither is a productive response when we are trying to get people to make decisions with the long-term success of our community in mind. The less heat that your elected officials feel, the more likely they are to make decisions and take actions aligned with the long-term priorities articulated in the plan.

RECOMMENDATION #3 – MAKE THEM CHEERLEADERS, NOT ACTIVE PARTICIPANTS

Some of your elected officials may feel a desire to become directly involved in the strategic planning process. By establishing an advisory committee to manage the process, you can go a long way in mitigating this tendency. Regardless, many elected officials seek office because they like to be involved. While you do not want to exclude elected officials from the process, it is not helpful to have them as direct participants.

Perhaps a story will illustrate. *In one community where I facilitated a community-based process, the advisory committee decided to host a community dialogue session in each of the council districts. They wanted to ensure that every resident felt like they had an easily accessible opportunity to participate and especially wanted to encourage involvement from areas of the community that had historically been less engaged. As a means of getting the word out, they contacted the elected official in each district and solicited their help in spreading the word about the meeting in their district. This was a great move as many elected officials have big e-mail lists that can be valuable in getting people out to these kinds of gatherings.*

Unfortunately, one of the meetings ended up going off the rails. The elected official in attendance took it upon himself to question and ultimately debate several of the points raised by citizens. This elected official had additional perspective to share and couldn't resist the chance to attempt to correct some misperceptions on the part of citizens. This caused some attendees at the meeting to disengage and left everyone that had participated with a bit of a bad taste in their mouths as they drove home that night. While the elected official was very accurate in his assertions, the purpose of the dialogue session was not to correct citizen understanding of issues. The purpose was to listen to citizen perspectives about their hopes for the future of the community.

The highest and best use for your elected officials in a community-based strategic planning endeavor is as supportive cheerleaders, not as players on the field. You need elected officials to champion and support the process, to encourage citizen participation, but not to dive into the process itself. As you find that you have elected officials that are eager to help, channel their energies towards those things that will drive increased citizen participation, not towards becoming active participants in the process themselves.

RECOMMENDATION #4 – SHARE REGULAR UPDATES

Communicate early and often about how the strategic planning process is progressing. This will serve two important ends. First, it will ensure that elected officials do not become overly involved in the process itself. When they know that things are moving along and feel "in the know" they will feel much less of a need to get overly involved and will trust the advisory committee to continue to manage the process. Second, by keeping them in the loop as things progress, it is much less likely that they will be surprised by anything that ends up in the strategic plan that the committee will present to them towards the end of the process.

For example, you can create a 5-minute agenda item every couple of months during a regularly scheduled meeting of the elected body and have a member of your SPAC provide a formal update. This does not need to be anything overly complicated, just a simple progress update where you put the timeline on the wall and let them know where you are in the process and provide some high-level observations about what has been learned so far.

CONCLUSION

Your elected officials have a tough job and often feel like they're in the line of fire. Help them see how a truly inclusive community-based planning process will help take some of the heat off of the elected body. Don't lose sight of the biological realities of serving in elected office and the sometimes-irrational behavior and decisions that those realities can create. Do everything you can to create safety and inspire trust in the process. Be sure that elected officials understand their role as key supporters and cheerleaders, but not drivers and implementers of the strategic planning process.

TAKEAWAYS

» *Remember that our brains are scanning for warmth and strength. In all of your discussions about the strategic planning process with elected officials, do everything you can to create safety, convey warmth, and build trust.*

» *Keep elected officials out of the process itself. It's for their own good as much as it is for the success of the planning process.*

» *Provide regular updates to the elected body as the planning process advances. This will help them trust the process and avoid any big surprises at the end.*

5

CITIZEN ENGAGEMENT

"If they don't weigh in, then they won't buy in."
— *Patrick Lencioni*

There is a scene portrayed in Lewis Carroll's *Alice in Wonderland* where Alice inquires of the Cheshire Cat which way she ought to travel. "Depends a good deal on where you want to go," said the Cat. "I don't much care where," said Alice. "Then it doesn't matter which way you go," said the Cat. " . . . So long as I get SOMEWHERE," Alice added as an explanation. "Oh, you're sure to do that," said the Cat, "if you only walk long enough."[15]

As we've mentioned, many well-intentioned individuals find themselves in public office with a firm determination to lead their community on a march forward sometimes without having given a tremendous amount of thought to where that march ought to lead, and more importantly where the people they are leading want to go. Like Alice, they may not be initially very concerned as long as they feel they are moving in

---

[15] Lewis Carroll, *Alice's Adventures in Wonderland* (London: MacMillan and Co., 1865).

some direction. **I wish I had a dime for every elected official that told me that their term in office ended up being nothing like they had imagined initially. I'm always curious to ask what they had imagined initially. Usually I get a response such as, "I thought we were going to be more unified." "I thought I would've seen our community coming together a little bit more than I did," is another common response.** It's not that most public officials lack good intentions. It's just that perhaps they haven't taken the time to unify people around a vision.

By now you likely understand that involvement of citizens in crafting a strategic direction is what sets community-based strategic planning apart from any other approach. Without community involvement, your journey as a public official is likely to become very much like Alice's. Remember our pixel example: the broader the base of public participation, the clearer and sharper the vision will be.

Since much of what your strategic planning committee will be doing is devising ways to engage your citizens, this chapter covers some of the ways to accomplish this. We are placing a lot of emphasis on the techniques used for engaging citizens in collecting feedback from them not only because it represents a critical element to community-based strategic planning, but also because it can be downright difficult to draw participation from your citizens, especially if they're not accustomed to engaging with their local government.

To illustrate this, let's talk about the most basic form of citizen interaction, voting. As most of you will probably attest, it is difficult to get even a sizable minority of your citizens to participate in local elections. In recent years, states and municipalities have designed and implemented a number of ideas intended to increase voter turnout. They've rescheduled municipal elections to coincide with national and state elections, increased the number of polling locations, mailed ballots directly to citizens (postage-paid), etc. Still, most communities are stuck around 20 percent in voter participation.

In one of my communities, we were experiencing a 10 to 15% voter turnout at municipal elections. Our clerk suggested that we move to an all-mail ballot. We would still have polling locations, just fewer of them and we would send a ballot to every residence. In addition, there would be plenty of publicity prior to the election informing citizens that they merely needed to fill out the ballot they would receive and drop it in the mail. The postage would be paid. If they still preferred to cast a ballot in person, they could do that. If they didn't trust the post office to deliver their ballot, they could fill it out and drop it by our offices. We could not have made this easier! As we celebrated a more than 30% participation in the next election using these new methods, I couldn't also help but think that 70% of our eligible voters wouldn't even make the effort to fill out a ballot at their kitchen table and drop it in the mail!

The first mistake that local governments make in the community-based strategic planning process is assuming that when they announce such an initiative, citizens are going to cry out for joy in one voice and participate in workshops and open houses by the thousands. If the past has taught us anything it is that it is not easy to engage citizens in local governance. Sure, you have that small group of involved citizens who have made local government a hobby, but the vast majority likely sit on the sidelines, perhaps blissfully disengaged. There are a variety of reasons why people don't feel the need to interact with local government. These may include their satisfaction with the way things are going, sheer apathy, a lack of confidence that their feedback will be taken seriously, the inhibition associated with interacting with people they don't know, or maybe their lives are so filled with family, career, and other priorities that it's downright difficult to focus on things outside of their immediate circle of concern. Whatever the reason, your job is to provide your citizens with *every* opportunity to participate in the strategic planning process. Let's discuss a few of the techniques that you may want to use.

Strategic Planning Branding

The brand of any organization or initiative is tied directly to what people think of it, if they are aware of it at all. The term "branding" pertains to what we *do* about what people think about our organization or initiative. As such pertains to strategic planning, it is critically important that your citizens understand a few basic things:

» *That your local government has decided to embark upon a community-based strategic planning process.*

» *That this process will include citizen input from every sector of your community.*

» *That their individual participation in helping create a strategic direction for the community is not only welcome but critical to the success of the project.*

Most people have a natural tendency to desire to be a part of ideas, movements, and endeavors that are "real" and bigger than themselves. To set the stage for citizen participation in strategic planning, residents are going to need to believe that the municipal government is serious about this endeavor. That's why the first and most important step in branding your strategic planning initiative involves elected official ratification of the process and appointment of a strategic planning advisory committee. These are very visible and official acts that will communicate immediately to citizens that you are serious about this endeavor. Beyond this, there are some things that you can do to increase the visibility of your initiative and encourage citizen participation.

First, following the elected body's appointment of a strategic planning advisory committee, it is advisable to meet with the SPAC to develop a communications strategy. Such a strategy should include development of a theme and catchy slogan and logo that can be quickly identified and tied to the strategic planning endeavor. One community, for example, decided to use the word "Imagine" in a variety of ways to communicate the mission of their strategic planning endeavor. This theme would actually bleed into another major community endeavor as they used the word "Imagine" for their community-wide branding campaign.

Another community determined that they would call their initiative "Envision 2020." If you want to get an example of other strategic planning slogans and logos, you could actually just search for those images on the internet. It isn't terribly important that your slogan and logo win you some type of marketing award. What's important is that it is something that can be used to quickly identify your strategic planning project. As you develop the slogan and image, make sure that it aligns well with your mission statement and that such is included as a part of all of your public communications and outreach.

Another key aspect of branding involves working with your local media. Spend some time with your designated beat reporter to develop his or her complete understanding of the strategic planning process and the results the community hopes to gain from this effort. You may want to additionally suggest to your local newspaper that they publish a strategic planning update from time to time. Usually, small local papers are very eager to work with staff and your strategic planning committee to provide regular updates and progress reports.

Meanwhile, your local government likely employs several means of communicating with citizens. It may use a website, newsletter, and even social media. My first recommendation is to meet with administration to determine your access to and usability of these media. A website, for example, is a wonderful place to establish a presence for your strategic planning initiative. Here you can not only administer online surveys, but also provide a consistent venue for public education associated with strategic planning and regular updates on the process. Likewise, if your local government publishes a newsletter, whether electronic or print, it is critical that you establish a strategic planning presence in that important medium. You may request to be allowed regular access and space to educate readers, encourage their participation in the process, and report progress. Finally, don't underestimate the power of social media.

We highly recommend that your strategic planning committee establish a Facebook page or leverage the local government's page where it can interact with citizens, educate, encourage, and report. Other social media such as Twitter can also be very powerful.

In addition, consider the following avenues for branding your initiative:

» *Other organizational newsletters (Chamber of Commerce, school district, PTO, etc.)*

» *Non-profit/service club meetings and newsletters*

» *Faith-based organizations*

» *Area newspapers*

» *Signage and banners*

» *County websites and newsletters*

» *Transit display advertising*

Examples of strategic planning logos

Methods for Gathering Public Input: The Orthodox and the Less Orthodox

This is where the real fun of strategic planning lives. In fact, it's also unfortunately where a lot of people want to begin without first having laid the foundational elements we have discussed up to this point. Obviously, when we contemplate how to gather public feedback, the first place everyone looks is to surveys. This is an important element that we will discuss a little later. Other more mainstream ways of gathering public input include open houses, workshops, and focus groups. All are very good ways to involve people, but we also want to take some time in this chapter to discuss some of the less common ways to get your citizens involved in strategic planning. To start however, let's talk about your stakeholders.

Stakeholders represent any group or organization that largely shares with you a mission or ambition and/or whose behavior, advocacy, or activities influence or have the potential of influencing your community. The most common stakeholder groups in a community are other governmental bodies such as the school district, the city, the county, or neighboring cities and towns. You will also want to include business groups, parent/teacher organizations, seniors, local government employees, and elected officials. Sometimes it's easy to forget some of the less obvious stakeholder groups such as children and youth, athletic organizations, arts councils, your legislative delegation, public safety organizations, community volunteer groups, healthcare providers, service clubs, and faith-based organizations. All are critically important to involve in the strategic planning process, and they can be of great assistance to you in gathering feedback and encouraging participation.

Just as doing some foundational work is critically important to the strategic planning process, so it is with gathering public feedback. Strategic planners who simply project themselves out to the community and expect that people will flock to their open houses and other public meetings are most times disappointed. This is why we suggest beginning with the formation of a stakeholder advisory subcommittee (SHAC). The purpose of this group is to assist the strategic planning committee with encouraging attendance/participation at strategic planning activities and events. The SHAC can also be a tremendous resource for identifying possible methods of communicating with stakeholder groups and granting access to mailing lists, email groups, and media that these organizations use to communicate with their membership.

Once you have identified the critical stakeholder groups in your community, it will be important for you to extend a personal invitation to the organization's leader to participate in planning the future of your community. This invitation is best extended by the SPAC chair with perhaps the additional assistance of the mayor. Our experience is that these types of community organizations generally embrace the opportunity to participate. Most immediately recognize the critical nature of planning the future of their community and easily see the nexus between such an activity and the health and future of their own organizations. As you approach each leader, tell them that you recognize and appreciate the important service that they provide and the valuable role they play in your community. Communicate your perspective regarding the importance of this initiative and invite either that person or an individual they designate to participate in perhaps two or three meetings to help develop the strategies for gathering citizen feedback. Finally, let them know that you would appreciate access to their membership as a means of ensuring that the strategic planning process is as inclusive as possible.

As you meet for the first time with the SHAC, spend some time getting each stakeholder group representative up to speed with the process of strategic planning, the timeline, and expected results. Also, take some time to make sure each organizational representative feels your enthusiasm for the initiative and its importance to your community. From there, allow the group to discuss in a brainstorming format how to best involve members of the community in the process. You may be very surprised at the kinds of ideas that surface.

Some years ago, I was taking a group through such an exercise when one of these stakeholder representatives from the local school district suggested several wonderful ways to involve children in the strategic planning process. One idea involved the local elementary schools' second grade classes. Children in each of the second grade classes could be assigned the task of visually portraying the future of that community. In fact, as the idea was actually implemented, it became a contest. Sometimes I believe kids embrace competition more readily than adults. In the end, a panel that included a teacher, the municipal manager, and the SPAC chair selected the best visual portrayal of their community's future by a boy and a girl. These kids received a prize and recognition at a council meeting. Meanwhile, the artwork of every pupil was displayed for several weeks at city hall. The drawings themselves provided the SPAC with valuable feedback about what kids hoped for in their community. Sure, there were plenty of drawings of Ferris wheels, merry-go-rounds, flying dolphins (as I recall), and a lot of other whimsical things; but the overall message was clear. These kids were very bullish on their community's future. There were few pictures of fires, collapsing buildings, lightning, or anything apocalyptic. These children saw a future that was full of optimism. And what do you think the exercise did in terms of spreading the word about the strategic planning initiative? Every parent and guardian of these children knew about the strategic planning endeavor in a very intimate way.

Before we move on to the discussion of data-gathering methodologies, allow us to make just a few more points about the stakeholder group. We're often asked if there are any hard or fast rules associated with who should serve on the SHAC. There are indeed a few pitfalls that you will want to avoid. First, those who serve on your stakeholder advisory committee truly need to represent real organizations or groups. We have found that there are times when the strategic planning committee staffs the stakeholder group with people who may have an intense interest in the strategic planning process and local government in general but who do not represent a real group or organization. Next, similar to membership on the strategic planning committee, stakeholder committee members should not only represent a true stakeholder group, but also be individuals who are not going to bring an overbearing ideology or political ambition to meetings. You cannot afford distractions and you do not want your meetings hijacked by people who have other ambitions. You're probably smiling right now, because you know of whom we speak. Every community has them.

Besides making sure that every stakeholder representative speaks for a true stakeholder group and is devoid of strong ideological ambition, there is another safeguard you can employ to ensure the purity of your group and its ability to contribute to the process. *Do not* invite a representative of any group of a political, ideological, or otherwise controversial nature. "But you're inviting faith-based organizations," you'll probably note. "Can't they be controversial?" Perhaps, but not as likely as groups who are politically or ideologically charged. It would be impossible for me to note every group you should or should not invite to be part of the stakeholder group without completely knowing your community. Therefore, my advice is to operate from this singular principle: avoid the inclusion of any individual or group on a committee who would likely draw unfavorable public attention to your strategic planning initiative and/or has shown the tendency in the past to dominate dialogue and hijack agendas. These are very difficult determinations to make sometimes. After all, the antithesis of what we are trying to achieve is alienation. However, you cannot take the chance of having your strategic planning endeavor turn into something narrowly focused on the pet projects of a few overbearing individuals.

Now, let's discuss a few of the more effective ways of gathering public feedback. These include surveys, workshops, open houses, and focus groups.

Surveys

Surveys are one of the most common instruments used by municipalities. Many communities expend considerable resources to regularly survey their citizens. The surveys usually focus on citizen satisfaction with departmental services. Typically, a consultant will be retained to ensure that public opinion is polled in a scientific manner which allows the approximation of an acceptable margin of error. Most of the time, anywhere from a 3 to 5% margin of error is regarded as acceptable. Providing this level of certainty regarding the results requires that a minimum number of citizens participate in the survey. This number depends on the total population of the community. A consultant will also ensure that the pool of survey participants is not only given an equal chance of participating in the survey, but also that they represent a fairly accurate cross-section of the community.

However, as it pertains to community-based strategic planning surveys, such criteria are generally unnecessary. The objective in a survey instrument used for strategic planning is to gather data from as many participants as possible. Because your survey is going to be far from the only instrument that you will utilize, it's not terribly important if more seniors than younger people participate, if more women fill out a survey than men, etc. What's critically important is that every one of your residents has the opportunity to chime-in. Another difference lies in the size of the survey that we will administer in a strategic planning project. While typical municipal surveys can be composed of 25 or more questions, we are going to concentrate on six very powerful questions. In fact, we are going to use these questions in not only our survey, but also in focus groups, workshops, open houses, and all other activities where we engage our citizens. The box on the following page articulates these questions.

The last primary difference between a scientifically controlled and validated survey and one that we are going to use for strategic planning pertains to the methods of gathering data. Traditional surveys may use mailers and the telephone to extract citizen opinions. This allows for analysis of respondent demographics. It is also very expensive. For a community-based visioning and strategic planning survey, we are going to put the survey on the local government's website and promote it heavily through every analog and digital media channel at our disposal. Use email lists to send potential participants links to the online survey. Make sure that your strategic planning committee makes an appearance at every community event during the planning process and distributes/gathers hard copies of the survey. Bottom line? Get this survey into as many of your citizens' hands as possible.

Our best advice: don't use a scientifically controlled and validated survey for a community-based strategic planning process. When you have something specific to ask your residents, go for statistical significance. In community-based strategic planning, however, you are not going for statistical significance, correlation coefficients, or anything of the sort. This is a qualitative instrument. You're trying to draw people out and get to the core of why they decided to move to this community and what sorts of things might cause them to leave. Also, your goal is to maximize the degree of participation. You want everyone in your community to get involved. Statistically valid surveys will exclude people, and the amount you will spend to develop and administer them could be better spent on conducting live workshops and focus groups to engage more citizens in the process.

The Six Most Powerful Strategic Planning Questions

1. What do you like most about_____?
2. Where would you like your [local government] to focus future efforts?
3. Why did you move to _____?
4. What would make you move from _____?
5. If you were in charge, what would you change about _____?
6. What other comments or insights do you want to share?

The first question allows us to probe the positive. Most residents do have warm feelings about their community, whether they relate to the natural beauty, fond family memories, a favorite store or restaurant, the color of the sunset, or any number of other possible characteristics. Our job with the first question is to capture the most prevalent positive feelings or characteristics associated with the community. As the plan evolves, citizen answers to this question provide an anchor and reality check. The last thing our committee wants to do is to make recommendations or create initiatives that eliminate or damage the things that people like most about the community.

The second question flows logically from the first. We want citizens to explain where they believe the community's priorities ought to lie. The third question probes the motivations behind their original decision to move to town. What was it that drew them there to begin with? Likewise, question four allows the citizen to explain what kind of change would represent a deal breaker for them and cause a decision to move. This question represents an effort to determine community priorities from a slightly different angle.

The fifth question is the typical "King or Queen for a Day" scenario. This is probably one of the most motivating questions that we ask. The sky is the limit! "We are going to give you absolute control over the destiny of your community. What would you do?" This is a powerful way to get to the heart of what they truly want to happen in their community. And if we haven't hit on every point or touched every nerve, the sixth question represents a very open ended method for allowing the participant to share any other insight that he or she believes relevant. Many times, the respondent will emphasize or repeat a point that they made when answering one of the previous questions.

The SPAC typically gets the final say on the design of the survey questions, but having a couple of questions that are not open-ended can facilitate analysis of the survey responses.

Meeting Facilitation

Before beginning a discussion of the different types of live outreach that you may consider, we would like to share some basic principles of meeting facilitation. These will help you in conducting workshops, open houses, focus groups or any other kind of live event where you solicit citizen input.

Meeting Length – In general, you should not go longer than 90 minutes with any meetings with citizens or other stakeholders. You want them to leave with a favorable impression of the community and excitement for the future. Keeping people too long is a great way to kill that excitement. So is failing to start on time. At the beginning of the meeting, let people know what time you will adjourn and then ensure that you end no later than that time. Our experience is that after about 120 minutes, people begin to lose focus, fatigue sets in, and the time spent on the exercise after this point becomes appreciably less productive. Resist the temptation to schedule a meeting much longer than about 90 minutes.

Meeting Cadence – Again, you are looking to leave a favorable impression and build excitement. Keep things moving. Keep people talking. If things start to wane, get people on their feet and moving around. Do whatever you can to keep things from dragging.

Group Size – You want to create plenty of opportunities for everyone to speak. As Pat Lencioni says, "If they don't weigh in, then they won't buy in." This means that if you have more than five or six people at the meeting, you will want to break people into smaller groups. Ideal group size is about five because it provides lots of opportunities for each member of the group to speak their mind.

> I once observed a community meeting where approximately 70 citizens turned out to share their thoughts. Unfortunately, the facilitator did not break the large group down into smaller groups. This meant that conversation was dominated by a few loud voices in the room and most of the people that attended

did not have an opportunity to speak. I spoke with several of the attendees as they were leaving and most felt disappointed that they had not had an opportunity to share their thoughts.

Don't make this mistake! You want to open up dialogue and discussion. You want to ensure that each participant has a chance to feel heard and understood. They should leave feeling like they had a part in setting the direction for the future of your community.

Workshops

Workshops represent one of the best means of gathering immediate feedback from large groups of people. Another advantage of this type of event is that participants generally have the opportunity to synergize ideas with each other and develop suggestions and solutions that may not have been possible to create through a survey. Workshops are also a great way of collecting larger groups of diverse people, since they are generally open to anyone; and they also represent an opportunity to educate citizens with regard to the strategic planning initiative, its purpose, and process.

The format for a typical workshop is simple. You'll need a large, open room. We found most success in cooperating with the local school district to arrange for a room at a middle school or high school. You can also use a community center, library, or any other building where people are going to feel comfortable. Next, make sure there are several large tables where groups of participants can sit comfortably. Supply each table with a stack of sticky notes and a Sharpie or other type of felt-tipped pen. In assigning or seating people, it will be important that you have no more than about eight people at each table (5 or 6 is ideal).

As we mentioned, punctuality is extremely important. If you have advertised the event to begin at 7 p.m., it is critically important that you begin promptly. You'll want to also tell participants when you expect the exercise to conclude and stick to that time frame. Generally speaking, the more participants, the longer the exercise is going to be. As a rule of thumb, we generally count on about 10–15 minutes of workshop time for every table or group of eight. That means that if you have 80 people at your workshop, you can probably count on at least an hour and a half. In no circumstances should you exceed two hours.

You will want participants seated at tables, whether round or rectangular, in a manner that allows them to face each other. A classroom configuration is not recommended. Remember, they are going to talk to each other more than they are going to listen to you. Next, make sure there is an area at the front of the room where you can fasten six large sticky notes so that they are visible to the group. Your instructions to the participants, meanwhile, are quite simple. You will explain that the municipality has decided to embark upon a community-based strategic planning exercise. Key to the success of this initiative is citizen participation in identifying community priorities. This project is being guided by a volunteer group of citizens who will take the information from surveys, focus groups, and workshops like this one and create a strategic direction for the local government which will be ratified by the elected body.

After you feel like participants have a pretty good grasp of what's going on, it's time to give them instructions. Tell them that they will work with other participants at their table to generate as many ideas as possible within an approximately 20–30 minute time frame. Inform them that they will need to designate one person (preferably somebody with legible handwriting) to write or transcribe the ideas onto sticky notes placed at each table, one idea per note. Inform the participants that they will be given one simple question and that they are free to generate, debate, and discuss as many ideas as possible within that 20–30 minute time frame. Also, ask them to designate a spokesperson for each table. Be sure to provide them with a couple of minutes of individual quiet time to jot down a few of their thoughts before you set them loose in their groups. This will generally have the effect of significantly improving the quality and thoughtfulness of the discussion.

As you begin the exercise, you will want to pose this question to the collective group: "If you were given the power to do so, what is it that you would change about this community?" You may want to explain further that ideas can include the addition of features or facilities currently not found in the community, the improvement or expansion of services, or any other thing they believe would most enhance quality of life. This is the "King or Queen for a Day" question. We ask this question because it generates the broadest range of responses. Of the six questions described previously, this question is really the juiciest when it comes to soliciting the greatest amount of creative feedback.

As workshop team members begin to interact with each other and write responses on sticky notes, you will want to take the opportunity to walk among the tables and observe these interactions. You'll also find that it is an excellent opportunity to clarify the instructions of the exercise and answer any other questions participants may have. In addition, and this is very critical, you'll want to do a little reading over the shoulder. As you do so, you'll begin to see patterns emerge at each table. Avoid the temptation to inject your bias into the discussions. For example, let's say that as you stroll around the room and both eavesdrop and read what is being said and written, you recognize at one particular table that the discussion involves items associated with economic development and transportation. Perhaps you see that other tables are discussing the same topics, in addition to perhaps public safety and recreation. These are great broad headings, but tuck those thoughts away for the moment. Once the groups have completed their work, have them select a spokesperson to share their sticky notes with the rest of the room. As they place their notes on the wall, encourage them to begin grouping them into broad overall categories. With each successive group that presents, these categories will become clearer. As the categories emerge, you can write a title above the grouping of sticky notes that relate to each category. In order to speed the process, you may want to begin by suggesting a category. For example, if the idea written on the sticky note is "build more restaurants," you may want to suggest "economic development" as the appropriate category and then confirm such with the group. Just be careful not to "lead the witness" too much. This is where the use of a professional facilitator can really help.

Keep in mind the value of applause. After the spokesperson has presented all of his or her group's ideas, invite all participants to express appreciation to this table with a round of applause. For whatever reason unknown to mankind, the clapping of one's hands has a great effect on all participants. It is a way of drawing the attention back into the activity, and it is an appropriate way of expressing appreciation for the efforts of those submitting their ideas. When people feel like their ideas, suggestions, and solutions are well received, there naturally emerges a desire to become even more engaged and to walk away from the experience with a very positive impression. When you are done, it's likely that you'll have 8 to 10 broad themes that organize the various sticky notes. *Example of workshop exercise. In one specific case, we actually assigned specific colored sticky notes to each table. This allowed us to identify which topics were the hottest within each subgroup.*

Once the exercise has concluded, take a step back from the sticky notes and ask your participants to tell you what they think the feedback tells them about the community's priorities. You may want to help them a little bit with this. **After one particular exercise, observing the emphasis that participants placed on both economic development and environmental sustainability, I stated something to the effect of, "I believe what you are saying is that you regard your community as a**

very unique, exceptionally beautiful place; and while you embrace growth and development and even welcome better access to goods and services, you believe and expect that such can be achieved in a manner that preserves the natural beauty of your community and even enhances that beauty." Not only did participants begin to nod affirmatively, but one participant stated that it was as though I was a longtime resident who completely understood their community. I didn't of course. THEY completely understand THEIR community. I simply translated what they expressed.

As we conclude the discussion of workshops and meander into the topic of focus groups, here are a few tips to consider in planning and conducting your workshops:

» *It's a good idea to have bottled water or other generally appreciated beverages on hand for participants. You may even want to provide some type of small snack item.*

» *Make sure the building is climatically friendly and that there is plenty of ventilation.*

» *Plan on holding a few workshops in various areas of your community. People will generally not travel great distances to participate. The more local it is, the greater your chance for participation.*

» *Stick around at the end of the workshop to answer questions. It's also a great time to get feedback that wasn't expressed during the exercise.*

» *Make sure at the end of the workshop to express sincere appreciation to those who took the time to participate in this important exercise. Be sure to express appreciation to the folks that made the room available as well.*

» *It will be very difficult for you to transport the large sticky notes without a few of the smaller sticky notes falling off or being dislodged. While they are still on the wall, take a photo of each one. These photos will allow you to transcribe that feedback into a form that will be more usable to the strategic planning committee. We have actually removed the small notes from the larger sticky notes, grouped them by category, and labeled them appropriately. Later on, we are then able to transcribe them by group into a table or other convenient format.*

» *Keep a tight grip on discussion. You don't want this to become an angry town hall meeting. Depending on the level of agitation and discontent in the community, there may be a tendency for the group to deviate from the purpose of the workshop. If you notice this occurring, remind the group that while you appreciate their passion for their community, the purpose of this event is more about what they would change in their community and less about debating the merits of those recommendations. The best way to keep participants on task is to make sure you are sticking to the script as described previously. If you begin to deviate, it is likely that your group will also. Avoid telling stories, talking about other communities, expressing your own opinions and political beliefs, or anything else that will derail your participants.*

Focus Groups

Many novice researchers will not be able to tell the difference between a workshop and a focus group. However, there exists a significant difference between these two methodologies. In short, a focus group is an exercise that involves a small group of individuals who share certain characteristics or association. Contrastingly, anyone could show up to a workshop, regardless of whether they share anything besides happening to live in the same community. A focus group is powerful because it is an intimate exercise where participants generally feel safer and more comfortable in expressing their opinions. Because the group is smaller, as a facilitator, you are able to pose all six of our strategic planning questions.

Generally speaking, you will want to limit focus groups to those stakeholders you believe to have a significant influence on your community. In a municipality, examples of these types of groups include local government employees, business owners, senior citizens, youth (13–18 years of age), volunteers, service or faith-based groups, ethnic groups, and developers. If a stakeholder group in your community is large and you believe that many members of that group have a desire to participate in the strategic planning process, this may signal the need to hold a workshop instead of a focus group. Then again, there is no rule that says you can't do both. What you don't want to do is alienate people who would have otherwise appreciated the chance to chime in.

Much like our workshop exercise, focus groups are best kept to groups of six or eight. It is important that participants feel comfortable with their surroundings and that they feel like you are there to listen to them. As is the case with workshops, it's appropriate for the facilitator to let the participants know of the purpose associated with the strategic planning initiative and how their feedback will be used. While some researchers insist on recording focus group sessions, for these sessions, we recommend that you leave the recorder at home. Make sure that you or someone else you bring to assist with the exercise is a good note taker. We have found that when people believe they are being recorded it inhibits their willingness to share things that are on their mind.

During the focus group exercise, you're going to present each one of the six strategic planning questions to the group. Make sure that each participant has an equal chance to share their thoughts. There may be a tendency on the part of one of your participants to dominate the discussion. If this occurs, address one of your other focus group members by name and ask for their specific feedback. This is kind of like blocking in a football game or setting up a screen in basketball. It clears the way for the less vocal to communicate.

At the end of the exercise, as we do with workshops, express sincere appreciation to those who participated. Just when to end a focus group discussion is dependent upon the level of conversation occurring. We liken it to making popcorn. You can always tell when to pull the popcorn out of the microwave because the popping becomes a lot less frequent. However, you don't want to wait until you hear no popping at all. That generally means burnt popcorn! Similarly, you don't want to end the focus group when every participant is exhausted and completely out of thoughts. When you look around the room and see that each person is glassy eyed and speechless, you've probably gone too far. Generally speaking, an hour is plenty of time for focus group discussion.

The power of a focus group is in the homogeneity of the participants. It's a chance to get a glimpse into the thoughts of people who represent a specific demography or association. Don't be dismayed or surprised at the homogeneous nature of some of the subjects that these groups surface. For example, it shouldn't surprise you that the senior citizens are going to want to talk about services that benefit primarily those over 65 years of age. Artistic people are going to want to talk about funding for the arts, while an ethnic group may want to focus on issues impacting them. All of this is okay. In fact, not only have you specifically broadened the base of participation by holding focus groups, but you have also provided an avenue for participation for people who perhaps were less likely to attend workshops or even less able to complete an online survey. Focus groups are a great way to bring legitimacy to the strategic planning process.

Now that we have discussed some of the more orthodox feedback gathering methodologies, we'll touch on some of the less orthodox ideas that we have encountered. You won't find any of them particularly bizarre, but these are the ideas that we have found most intriguing and effective.

Youth Involvement

Many communities struggle over how to involve young people in their strategic planning process. Children and young adults represent a very valuable segment of any community. Clearly the reason we are even engaging them in strategic planning is to provide a higher quality of life for them and *their* children. It is therefore imperative that we tap this resource. Young people can offer a perspective and vision for the future that older residents are less able to provide. They tend to have less inhibition in sharing their vision; and by their very nature, they are futuristic and visionary.

One of the more effective ways to involve young people is through a competition or contest that offers recognition for the winner(s). **In the first community that I assisted through the strategic planning process, as mentioned earlier in this book, second graders of the community were asked by the strategic planning committee to artistically present their perspectives of the future of their community. This was a huge success and the committee benefited from the perspective that few other stakeholder groups could have provided.**

Another idea we have seen employed involves teenage youth. In one community, the strategic planning committee sponsored an essay contest, with the advice and consent of local junior high school educators. The topic was "What the future holds for my community." Several dozen youth participated in the contest, and once again the committee received valuable perspective specific to what these young people hoped for and even feared. Yet another local government reached out to their older youth at the high school level and challenged them to create short 2–4 minute videos depicting what they thought the future held for their community.

In each case, male and female winners were chosen by the strategic planning committee, appropriate recognition was provided by the elected body, and each winner received a small gift, prize, or other recognition. So important was the youth component to one Arizona community that they actually appointed a high school student to serve as a member of their strategic planning committee.

Community Events

Ask nearly any mayor or municipal manager in the United States what event draws the most people together in her community, and 9 times out of 10 it will be something to do with Independence Day. Other communities see their largest crowds at other celebrations that commemorate the founding or heritage of the community. Still other communities host large athletic and cultural events. Whatever the occasion, your strategic planning committee should not miss the opportunity for visibility and interaction with citizens at these events.

One tactic involves the strategic planning committee reserving booth space at fairs, carnivals, expositions, or other public events. If there are people gathered in any general location, your committee should be visible. Such events not only provide an opportunity to interact and educate, but they also provide a chance to distribute hard copies of your survey and gather feedback from event attendees. Remember, you only have six questions to ask. That can be done very quickly at almost any venue and at any time. A larger community we worked with actually distributed the surveys along a parade route prior to the parade. By the time they worked their way down the line of people on each side of the street, they worked their way back collecting the completed surveys. Another committee set up a table at a "Meet the City Night" that the local municipality was sponsoring. As people filed in through the door to meet and visit with their local government officials, they were greeted at the door by a strategic planning committee member and a survey. Receptacles were placed around the building to collect completed surveys. Yet another community found success in setting up booths at a fair hosted by the school district marking the end of the school year. As you begin your strategic planning project, it would be very wise to sit down with your local government's event planner to calendar potential feedback-gathering opportunities. We have never encountered a local government that did not go out of its way to accommodate this type of data gathering. In fact, very much like the "Meet the City" event, some municipalities have even invented opportunities to bring people together for feedback collection.

Allowing the Business Community to Help

Unfortunately, many communities make the mistake of failing to recognize their businesses as residents of the community. While a typical resident may have made a financial commitment to your community in the form of a home, many businesses have invested millions. They have a tremendous amount riding on the success of your community. They should therefore applaud your efforts to create a community blueprint for the future. Not only that, but you will nearly always find that they are enthusiastic about helping out. Most businesses understand the necessity of planning. Those businesses that don't develop and follow a business plan generally aren't around very long. The concept of strategic planning is in its very essence a principle and practice borrowed from the private sector. With the clamor that has existed over the last several decades demanding that government become more like business, most of your community's businesses will applaud your strategic planning efforts.

Your local chamber of commerce is probably the best place to start. We'll address a little later what you can do if your community doesn't have a chamber. Meanwhile, for those communities that do, don't underestimate the reach and capabilities of this business group. In most places, the chamber represents the primary association of businesses in the community. Chambers hold events, maintain email lists, perform business retention visits, and provide a host of other valuable services into which your strategic planning committee can and should tap.

Right up front, you should involve your local chamber and strategize with them to hold and organize focus groups, distribute and collect surveys, and assist the SPAC with branding the strategic planning initiative. For example, in another larger community, a number of door decals were distributed to businesses that sported the strategic planning logo and slogan. Inside many of the businesses, a customer could complete a strategic planning survey and leave it with the business. Many patrons found that they had plenty of time to complete a survey while they waited for their "take and bake" pizza or their Chinese food. Likewise, service centers, especially those that require some wait time, are excellent venues for strategic planning surveys.

For those of you who don't have a chamber in your community, you'll have to do a bit more legwork. Plan for some time to visit your largest employers or more prominent retailers. It may make sense to bring the mayor. She can speak authoritatively and probably passionately about the strategic planning process and its importance to the community. Also, take a little time to brainstorm with these business owners about ways that they can assist in the strategic planning process.

Community Branding

Some municipalities take advantage of the strategic planning process to revisit their entire branding strategy. As I mentioned before, your community's brand can have a tremendous impact on your local government. If your community is considering refreshing its logo, launching an economic development marketing campaign, developing a new slogan, refreshing the website, or any number of other visible initiatives, it may make sense to marry that endeavor with the strategic planning process. By so doing, you magnify your ability to draw attention to it.

Community branding endeavors, mostly because they are so visible, attract a lot of attention. Such also allows your municipal government to involve citizens, in a limited way, in remaking the community image. In West Jordan, Utah, for example, the city decided to expand the use of the theme associated with their strategic planning process, "Imagine West Jordan," and crafted a community marketing campaign around it. They even produced a short marketing video about their community, carrying the same theme, which was used widely in their economic development recruitment efforts. To this day, a drive through West Jordan will reveal dozens of city banners bearing the theme that had its genesis in the strategic planning process.

CONCLUSION

The success of your strategic planning initiative depends largely on your ability to broaden and maximize participation in creating your community's priorities. Just like the number of pixels in a television, your strategic direction will become clearer as you increase the number of people who participate by providing their feedback. It is critically important in the beginning of the process that the strategic planning committee and the strategic planning initiative be ratified by the governing body. Also critically important is the development of a communications plan and project brand. Such efforts can and should include identifying appropriate methods for communicating the initiative's mission, schedule, and expected benefits to the community, as well as tying the endeavor to an easily identifiable logo or slogan. The key is to ensure that this project is seen as something that is real and important to the local government.

There are meanwhile a variety of ways that have been shown to be effective in maximizing public participation in the strategic planning process. These methods include both the orthodox and the creative. An important first step to developing data gathering methods is to identify stakeholder groups and invite their involvement. These groups can be very effective in developing ways to both communicate with their memberships and maximize member participation. Traditional methods of gathering public feedback include surveys, workshops, and focus groups. The objective in administering a strategic planning survey is to maximize the number of people completing the survey. Generally, strategic planning surveys are administered through the local government's website (often with the help of third-party survey tools), emailed to citizen and stakeholder groups, and provided in hard copy form at times and in places where citizens are likely to gather. Workshops can be held in various locations throughout your community where there is room enough to accommodate a large gathering of people. Focus groups can be conducted with small groups that share common objectives, interests, and influence.

Less traditional data-gathering activities may include strategies to involve children and young adults through contests and competitions. Other techniques may involve synergizing efforts with the business community, taking advantage of community events, and linking strategic planning with a broader community marketing initiative. With the mission and objective of maximizing public input and participation, there exists no end of ways to involve your citizens. Creativity is the only limit.

TAKEAWAYS

» *The more you involve your citizens and engage them in strategic planning, the clearer and sharper the direction that you need to take your community will be.*

» *The first mistake that local governments make in the community-based strategic planning process is assuming that when they announce such an initiative citizens are going to cry out for joy in one voice and participate in workshops and open houses by the thousands. If the past has taught us anything it is that it is not easy to engage your citizens in local governance. Your job is to provide your citizens with every opportunity to participate in the strategic planning process.*

» *It is advisable to meet with the SPAC to develop a communications strategy. Such a strategy should include developing a theme and catchy slogan and logo that can be quickly identified and tied to the strategic planning endeavor.*

» *The purpose of the stakeholder advisory committee (SHAC) is to assist the strategic planning committee with encouraging attendance/participation at strategic planning activities and events. The SHAC can also be a tremendous resource for identifying possible methods of communicating with stakeholder groups and granting access to the mailing lists, email groups, and media that these organizations use to communicate with their memberships.*

» *The objective in a survey instrument used for strategic planning is to gather data from as many participants as possible. Because your survey is going to be far from the only instrument that you are going to utilize, it's not terribly important if more seniors than younger people participate, if more women fill out a survey that men, etc. What's critically important is that every one of your residents has the opportunity to chime-in.*

» *Workshops represent one of the best means of gathering immediate feedback from large groups of people. Another advantage of this type of event is that participants generally have the opportunity to synergize ideas with each other and develop suggestions and solutions that may not have been possible to create through a survey.*

» *Many communities make the mistake of failing to recognize their businesses as residents of the community. Right up front, you should involve your local chamber and strategize with them to hold and organize focus groups, distribute and collect surveys, and assist the committee and municipal government with branding the strategic planning initiative.*

6

INTERPRETING CITIZEN FEEDBACK AND CREATING STRATEGIC DIRECTIVES

"The only thing worse than being blind is having sight but no vision."
— Helen Keller

When I was a teenager, a friend of mine and I enjoyed occasionally traveling into nearby San Francisco. Even though we were local, we liked to walk around tourist-oriented locations like Pier 39, Fisherman's Wharf, and stop in for an ice cream sundae at Ghirardelli's. During one such excursion into the city, we came across a very curious sight. You're probably laughing at this point because there are many curious sights in San Francisco; but this one particularly caught our attention.

A retailer had attached one of those 3D computer-generated posters to the front of his store. These are the images where you have to gaze deeply into the picture, cross your eyes a bit, lift one leg, etc., in order to see the hidden image concealed deep within the picture's landscape. When you first look at it, it simply appears chaotic.

However, some people are actually able to adjust the way they look at the picture so that the true image appears in three dimensions.

My friend was already, at the age of 18, a pretty accomplished artist. He can pick up the least bit of detail in architecture, paintings, you name it. I am not an artist, and am quite a bit less able to pick up such subtleties. He was very quick to see the three-dimensional object hidden in the picture attached to the store front door. Determined, I stood there with my eyes fixed on that picture for what seemed to be hours while I listened to him "oooooh" and "aaaahhh." It was actually quite a frustrating experience, even though several times I thought I had actually glimpsed the hidden object.

We compare the process of interpreting citizen feedback to the 3D poster experience in San Francisco. You've got a lot of data that you've gathered from every corner of your community. Now what? Do you simply slap it up on a wall and hope that you see the three-dimensional object behind all of the data? Well, sort of. We say "sort of" because you are going to be looking for what's behind the façade of the data. You're going to need to determine what people are *really* saying.

To begin the process of interpreting the results of your data-gathering exercises, you'll need to make sure that the information you've collected is put into a format that is most easily read and interpreted. Information from the citizen survey, for example, can certainly be put into charts and graphs. You'll also want to make the raw responses available to the strategic planning committee. Information that you gather from workshops and focus groups can be formatted into tables or other narratives. The key is to begin by making the data as easy to interpret as possible so that your strategic planning committee can avoid standing there staring at the data hoping that they catch a glimpse of the hidden three-dimensional object. Particularly for larger communities, an outside consultant can really help at this stage of the process because they have already spent a lot of time staring at those 3D posters and can relatively quickly create a more digestible summary of key observations that will keep your SPAC from having to spend dozens of hours poring over the data.

For those who have never gone through the process of interpreting citizen feedback, it can be a bit daunting. That's why we're going to suggest a few techniques that will significantly simplify the data interpretation process. However, before we move to that subject, allow me to explain what we're going to be doing with the results of our data analysis.

The first portion of the strategic plan that your committee will compose is in fact the plan's strategic directives. A directive is a very broad description of a citizen priority. All of your data collecting over the course of all of those weeks and months has been accomplished almost entirely with the purpose of allowing you to identify these broad citizen priorities. The strategic directives are critical because all other initiatives and ideas articulated in the plan will be organized around these directives.

So how do we take all of the data collected from surveys, workshops, focus groups, etc. and translate them into citizen priority areas? The first key is to relax. As you read this, without having gone through such an experience before, it may seem an impossible task. However, you'll have to trust us on this one. By the time you and your committee have successfully executed all of the data-gathering events and activities, looked at the results of the survey, and probably spoken with dozens and dozens of citizens, you are extremely likely to have a very good idea of what primary themes are coming to the surface. Actually, citizens in almost every community share with each other some pretty fundamental concerns. In almost every community with which we have worked, citizen feedback could generally be grouped into five or six general areas:

- » *Financial sustainability and responsibility*
- » *Youth and children*
- » *Transportation and other infrastructure*
- » *Economic prosperity and development*
- » *Public safety*

» *Community amenities (parks, trails, open space, arts, events, etc.)*

It is a safe bet that your community will have similar priorities. Where you will deviate a great deal from other local governments is in the way that you articulate those directives and in the initiatives you create under each directive. A little more on that later. Before we go there, let's go back to your survey.

We mentioned that the information from your citizen survey can be displayed visually in charts and graphs. However, we were being a little simplistic. If you administer a survey electronically through your website or any other way, it's likely that you are using a program such as SurveyMonkey. This is a pretty useful tool for electronically administering your survey. It allows you to format your questions in a variety of ways and tabulate the results. The problem is that SurveyMonkey cannot delve very deeply into a survey participant's feedback in order to bring to the surface an interpretable response. Perhaps an example here is helpful.

Consider the following response from one community's citizen questionnaire. As you read, keep in mind that the question to which the participant is responding is "Where would you like the city to focus future efforts?"

> **"This town is growing so fast. Which is good, but if the town can't keep up with the growth, it is very inconvenient for people who live here. For example, traffic lights are needed in various areas and the town is unable to put them in in a timely manner, so as a result we will have car accidents, hopefully no deaths. To me, this seems to be a big problem. I hope the city will address it. Especially down there by the middle school and the elementary. You can't feel safe taking your child to school."**

Did you catch the answer? You probably did, but SurveyMonkey didn't. The answer here to the question of where the city should focus future efforts is "managing growth." It really isn't singularly about traffic lights, safe walking routes for children, or even vehicle accidents. What this respondent wants is the town to focus future efforts on managing growth in a manner that provides an adequate level of safety on several different levels. Again, it would be very difficult for a computer program to have interpreted this correctly and appropriately categorized the answer (even IBM Watson). Additionally, many of your survey answers are going to arrive in paper form.

That's why there is no shortcut when it comes to pulling responses from your surveys. Someone is going to have to read every response from the open-ended questions that you present to your citizens. There is no automated way to do this. And before we go any further, please believe us when we say that we feel your pain. We have read thousands of survey responses. What's more, it can often be necessary to read through responses twice before it is possible to accurately categorize survey results. However, with pain comes wisdom. After such effort, there are very few individuals who know the citizens of these communities better than we do. Although it takes some time to work your way through survey responses and individually categorize them, you will come to understand your citizens in a way that would be quite difficult to match any other way. This will certainly empower you when it comes to the task of creating the strategic directives.

We're often asked whether we have any keys or tricks associated with how to categorize survey data. First, we suggest that you begin with a finite number of broad categories, such as those suggested previously. If you think it appropriate, add more. We may also suggest using a spreadsheet or table to capture and record the data. We have even known of individuals who have simply written the category headings down one side of a piece of paper, recording frequencies to the right of those categories with hash marks in groups of five; kind of the way a medieval dungeon prisoner would mark the passing of time. If you are using Survey Monkey, that program has an interesting feature that allows the user to create something called "Word Clouds." Word clouds focus on key words or terms used in survey responses and then portray these words or terms in a size reflective of frequency of use. We've provided an example of such a word cloud below.

What do you like most about our community?

Access Air Beauty Clean Parks Recreation
Community Country Fact Family View
High Density Housing Lake Living Location
Low Density Not Overly Open Space Quiet
Running Rural Safety Schools Slower Pace
Small Town Transportation
Neighborhood Close to the City

This word cloud was produced to illustrate the frequency of words contained in responses to the question about what citizens liked most about their community. In this case, you can see that "neighborhood" dwarfs other responses. In fact, the data clearly show that the residents of this city very much appreciate the safety, cleanliness, and friendliness of their individual neighborhoods.

Word clouds are not only helpful in identifying common themes, but they are an excellent method for presenting information to a third-party audience. It's a quick way to get a very real sense of what people are saying. However, regardless of the type of illustration you choose, don't get lost in the methods so much that you forget the principle. The task at hand is to group survey responses in a way that allows your strategic planning committee to begin creating the strategic directives.

This is a good time for another example. Actually, we will run this example all the way through the creation of a hypothetical strategic plan.

Creating Strategic Directives

We will assume for this example that you have examined the findings of your citizen survey, pored through the myriad responses from your workshops and focus groups, and analyzed answers provided to you from citizens at various venues and events during the data gathering phase. As a result, you and your committee have identified the following broad priorities:

» *Public safety*

» *Parks, trails, and open space*

» *Recreation*

» *Municipal infrastructure*

» *Senior services*

» *Planning and development*

» *Municipal services*

» *Retail development*

» *Neighborhood aesthetics*

» *Environmental sustainability*

» *Youth programs*

» *Community health*

» *Financial responsibility*

» *Arts and events*

» *Local government responsiveness and customer service*

» *Citizen communications*

» *Community*

» *Transportation*

» *Taxes and fees*

» *Job creation*

Your committee believes that these broad categories capture the greatest portion of citizen feedback during the data gathering phase.

In other words, most feedback provided to you from citizens will find a home in one of these categories, regardless of whether that feedback came from a survey, focus group, workshop, or any other data gathering exercise. These are the themes that you notice surfacing, perhaps quite early in data gathering. They are the things that you kept hearing citizens say. They are also the raw materials from which we will craft our strategic directives.

The first step is to see if any of these can be combined or brought together to create an expanded category or a different category altogether. As you glance at the list above, I'm guessing you can already see some commonality and potential for combining categories. For example, "local government responsiveness and customer service" could be combined with "citizen communications." Meanwhile, "municipal infrastructure" could be merged with "transportation." "Public safety" could also be combined with "community health," and so on and so forth. Let's now assume that your committee has been able to condense these 20 categories into the following list:

   » *Community health and safety*
   » *Economic and community development*
   » *Local government responsiveness and customer service*
   » *Fiscal responsibility and sustainability*
   » *Infrastructure*
   » *Aesthetics and environmental sustainability*
   » *Sense of community*

From this example, we see that we now have seven broad categories or priorities. A little caution here, don't try to hurry your committee through this exercise. You are likely to enjoy quite a bit of lively discussion as you begin to synthesize your data into strategic directive categories. That only means that you're doing it correctly. It should not necessarily be easy to condense everything that you've learned over the last several months of data gathering into perhaps 6 or 7 categories.

You should also know that there is no one "right" answer in doing this. Using the list above, reasonable people could disagree about how to organize the directives. For example, some might argue that recreation and youth programs is really just a component of "sense of community." It is also important to note that there is no magic number of directives. Having said that, if you have 10 strategic directives, you probably have too many. Too many directives will dilute the focus and utility of a strategic plan. If you have 2 or 3, you probably have too few. Most plans end up with 5 or 6. You should also keep in mind that the SPAC will ultimately determine which items merit consideration as strategic directives and which items may not make the final cut. There is a significant element of subjectivity in this evaluation. However, if you have put together a solid process, and gathered lots of data points (pixels, to use our earlier example) from a good cross section of the community, the big themes will be hard to miss. The less significant items will fade into the background of the picture.

How you format your directives is really up to you and your committee. Generally speaking, each directive should be articulated in a manner that captures the essence of each priority. Keep in mind that you want to articulate these directives in a way that they are accessible to the residents of your community. This means that you should generally avoid municipal management jargon to the extent possible. One of the first communities we assisted through the strategic planning process decided to state each directive as if it were a desire being articulated by a citizen. For example, when it came to public safety, SPAC members described their directive as follows:

"I want to live in a place where my family feels safe."

That's it and that's all. The plan went on to explain what this statement meant:

**"This strategic directive speaks to the need to foster a
safe environment where neighborhoods are walkable at all**

hours, quiet, and clean, where there is a sense of shared ownership and personal responsibility for the safety and appearance of our city."

Wow! This community equates community aesthetics and cleanliness with safety. Doesn't that make perfect sense? It absolutely *does*. There are many studies that show that code enforcement and neighborhood beautification have tremendous effects on reducing crime in a community. Bravo to this committee for recognizing the corollaries here!

Another community decided to both articulate the directive and follow it with a value statement. When it came to Directive 1, the strategic planning committee stated:

"In [our community], we value a strong sense of community. We seek to build and nurture this by providing opportunities for citizen participation in local governance and planning, problem solving, and volunteerism. Communication between citizens and local government is clear, abundant, diverse, and transparent. We take advantage of opportunities to further build our sense of community through celebrations of our community's heritage, participation in local activities/events, and by investing in the quality of our city and neighborhoods."

The associated value statement goes on to describe this directive as speaking to the importance of consistently engaging citizens in both community work and play. It explains that citizens want to feel pride and ownership in their local government, and want to be involved and informed. To conclude, the committee states that their community values their heritage and that citizens share the responsibility for building a bright future.

From our own example, we are now going to work on creating our own strategic directives using our list of categories on the previous page. This is really where the strategic planning committee begins to "earn their money" as it were. Before composing our strategic directives, we are going to ask and answer four basic questions with regard to each category:

> » *What are citizens saying and what are we as committee members noticing?*
> » *What is occurring that we like?*
> » *What is occurring that we don't like?*
> » *Where are the primary deficiencies?*

Let's take the first hypothetical category "community health and safety" and work this one through to the creation of a strategic directive:

COMMUNITY HEALTH AND SAFETY

What are citizens saying and what are we noticing?

We have noticed through our research that citizens appear to be quite concerned about the aesthetic appearance of our community and how that relates to the potential for crime. They have complained about the state of some of the deteriorating neighborhoods in the southern part of the community and suspect that these neighborhoods have become a breeding ground for criminal activity and mischief. Many citizens have complained that response times from police have been long, and they worry that the community has not adequately maintained a level of law enforcement consistent with the growth in the area. As committee members, we concur with the citizen feedback and have additionally noted a lack of safe walking routes for schoolchildren. We have also noticed the absence of traffic signalization at several dangerous intersections.

What do we like?

Citizens expressed appreciation for police courtesy and have noticed the little extra things that our officers have done to assist citizens. Citizens have also noticed that the downtown area appears to be clean and well-maintained, and they feel safe shopping in the urban center. They expressed appreciation for the fire department's public education efforts, and most still perceive that their community enjoys a low crime rate. As a committee, we recognize our officers and firefighters as exceptionally professional, well-trained, and dedicated public servants. Equipment appears to be new/modern and public safety personnel appear appropriately deployed throughout the community.

What is occurring that we don't like?

Citizens are worried that the local government is not maintaining staffing stasis with the area's growing population. Deteriorating neighborhoods are becoming hotbeds for crime, while children are forced to walk in the road right-of-way to school, especially during the winter months when the snow drifts occupy the shoulders of roads. Lighting appears insufficient in many areas, inviting both crime and auto/pedestrian accidents. Citizens are concerned that their community property values will slide as they lose their reputation for being a safe, clean, family-oriented community.

Where are the deficiencies?

Code enforcement is inadequate, especially in southern neighborhoods. The local government has not made an adequate investment in maintaining infrastructure in the southern area of the community. These deficiencies have signaled to criminals that it is safe to begin operating in these neighborhoods. Lighting is insufficient along school walking routes, as are sidewalks. Both local and state controlled intersections require signalization. Citizens are additionally concerned that police and firefighter staffing, not to mention dedications to advanced life support (ALS), have not been adequate to accommodate growth in the community.

From the preceding answers to our four questions, we are now ready to begin the composition of a strategic directive. In doing so, it is important to keep in mind that a strategic directive is not a restatement of the problem. It is the articulation of the ideal. In other words, our strategic directive is going to say what we *want* to happen. Let's try it out with our Community Health and Safety directive. Given all we know, all we've

RICK DAVIS AND DAN GRIFFITHS

heard, and all we've learned, here is an example of what our first directive in this hypothetical plan may look like (for the purposes of this example, the name of our community will be Metro City):

> **"Metro City is a healthy and safe community. As such, we work together to build and maintain neighborhoods that contribute to the quality of our community. Ours is a community that is walkable at all hours and that provides multiple and safe means of transportation. Police and fire are staffed with dedicated personnel and provided the best equipment to meet the demands of our growing community."**

Additional language could be added to this directive to further explain the community values supporting this priority, as follows:

> **"In Metro City, community health and safety is foundational to quality of life. We therefore regard the investment in elements that contribute to health and safety as the paramount responsibility of citizens and their local government. We expect all community members to work together to ensure the safety of our citizens by supporting this investment and by maintaining our neighborhoods as safe and healthy places for individuals and families."**

It doesn't get any more straightforward than that. Metro City has made a declaration. It will not tolerate the deterioration of any part of the community, a lack of pedestrian safety, dangerous intersections, and inadequately staffed and equipped emergency personnel. Citizens expect that their community will continue to be a safe place to raise a family and enjoy a high quality of life. As we get into the creation of strategic initiatives, we will see how the strategic planning committee can begin to prescribe broad methods, ideas, and strategies to meet these deficiencies, or in better words, bring this strategic directive to fruition.

For now, however, it should be clear that you are going to take every one of your broad strategic categories through this process that we illustrated with Community Health and Safety. You will answer each of the four questions as thoroughly and completely as you can. Again, do not hurry this process. Just like building a house, you are laying the foundation of the plan. If you don't spend enough time on the foundation, the rest of the plan may become unstable and eventually collapse. *Make absolutely sure that your committee is as unified as possible in the creation of your strategic directives.* Dissension and a lack of unity are absolute poison when it comes to the creation of your strategic plan. That doesn't mean that you need unanimity, but you need to get as close to it as possible.

SPAC Prerogative

On a final note, we should touch just briefly on the prerogative of the strategic planning committee. If you find yourself on this committee or you are an elected/appointed administrative official, it is imperative to understand and explain to committee members that they have been empowered by the elected body to not only collect feedback from citizens, but also exercise their privilege to include elements, priorities, or ideas that weren't necessarily articulated by citizens. In other words, if the strategic planning committee believes that the citizens have not clearly or adequately emphasized a priority that the committee believes ought to be part of the plan, SPAC members can and should insert that element for consideration by the elected body.

In one Arizona city with whom Rick worked, the SPAC determined that "civility," in terms of how citizens treated each other, should be a community priority or directive. The committee also saw ways the city could encourage and nurture a spirit of civility in their community. While it had not been clearly articulated as a citizen priority, the strategic planning committee believed it an important enough element to include in their draft plan. The elected body actually ratified the plan with that directive included, and for good reason. Not only had they (the elected body) become mostly dysfunctional because of their own deteriorating relationships, but they also saw significant dissension and lack of respect in the community, citizen to citizen, becoming a major stumbling block for progress. Had the committee not seen the need and exercised their prerogative to include civility as a community priority, it would have never been addressed by the strategic plan.

Therefore, take heart in the fact that your elected body has trusted its strategic planning committee members to exercise this discretion. On the flipside, the committee may also filter citizen feedback to ensure that the plan remains a relevant document for the next five years. Allow us to provide an example.

One community had become a candidate site for a state prison re-location. As fate would have it, this revelation came to light during the strategic planning data gathering phase. There were very few other things that citizens rejected as strongly as the idea of becoming the home of a new state prison. They saw every aspect of their quality of life evaporating if the prison came to town. During data gathering, we saw this reaction woven throughout every citizen response. In fact, citizen feedback was literally peppered with the word "prison."

Meanwhile, the decision relative to the prison's location was left in the hands of a small committee commissioned by the state legislature. Within a matter of a few weeks, this community had been dropped from the list as a possible site. You may be able to see how it would have been a mistake to include the prison issue in a strategic directive. It was a very temporarily heated issue with little relevance to this community beyond the immediate future, much less five years from now when that community would want to revisit the strategic plan. The strategic planning committee was able to filter that issue out of citizen feedback and concentrate on the truly impactful elements.

You may likewise find in your process that some temporarily hot issue will emerge during your data gathering phase. These types of issues often make people think that the world is coming to an end. To identify and filter these types of issues out, ask yourself "While important now, is this something that will be important or relevant a few months or even a few years into the future?" Another community experienced the first earthquake to shake the town in the last several decades. While the quake didn't cause a significant amount of property damage and there was no human collateral loss or harm, many citizens thought that their strategic plan ought to address earthquake preparedness. My guess is if they had included it, after the issue cooled and memories faded, someone would have questioned why earthquake preparedness had risen to the level of a community priority. Ultimately, they did not include it as a directive, but appropriately listed emergency preparedness as a strategic initiative under a broader public safety directive.

Whether your strategic planning committee has added a priority or filtered out citizen input, it should clearly disclose such instances to the governing body. This is most appropriately done as you report progress to the elected body or provide them with the first draft of the plan. Your elected officials need to clearly see where the committee has exercised its prerogative.

CONCLUSION

At the conclusion of the data gathering phase, the strategic planning committee will begin the process of synthesizing the data collected into community priorities, also referred to as strategic directives. A strategic directive is a clear and concise articulation of a community priority. The committee can utilize any one of a number of methods to portray and illustrate the data collected from citizens. This analysis should allow the strategic planning committee to begin categorizing issues into broad priority categories. The SPAC can then begin to condense these categories into a finite number of categories. In order to begin forming a strategic directive, the committee will take each priority category and ask and answer four primary questions: 1) What are citizens saying about this and what do we as a committee notice? 2) What is going right? 3) What is it that we see going wrong? and 4) Where are the deficiencies?

Each directive ought to be stated as an expectation that reinforces the good and addresses deficiencies. In developing strategic directives, the committee may exercise its prerogative to include directives that were not communicated by citizens. The committee may also filter citizen feedback to exclude non-relevant elements. Such may include the exclusion of feedback that is tied to a short-term issue. It is critical that the committee make it very clear to the governing body when and how they exercise this prerogative.

TAKEAWAYS

» *To begin the process of interpreting the results of your data-gathering exercises, you'll need to make sure that the information you've collected is put into a format that is most easily read and interpreted.*

» *By the time you and your committee have successfully executed all of the data-gathering events and activities, looked at the results of the survey, and spoken with dozens and dozens of citizens, you are extremely likely to have a good sense of what primary themes are coming to the surface.*

» *Make absolutely sure that your committee is as unified as possible in the creation of your strategic directives. Dissension and a lack of unity are absolute poison when it comes to the creation of your strategic plan. That doesn't mean that you need unanimity, but you need to get as close to it as possible.*

» *If the strategic planning committee believes that the citizens have not clearly or adequately provided a priority that the committee believes ought to be part of the plan, SPAC members can and should insert that element for consideration by the elected body. The SPAC may also filter citizen feedback to ensure that the plan remains a relevant document for the next five years. When your strategic planning committee has added a priority, or filtered out citizen input, it should clearly disclose such instances to the governing body. Your elected officials need to clearly see where the committee has exercised its prerogative.*

7

CREATING THE PLAN

———

"The difference between something good
and something great is attention to detail."
— Charles R. Swindoll

One of the greatest personal deficiencies with which I have been forced to grapple in my life involves my lack of direction. This is not a reference to an inability to know who I am and where I'm going in life. No, I mean that I literally have a tough time finding my way from point A to point B in my car. I have therefore purchased and installed various types of navigational devices. My wife, Aimee, on the other hand appears to have been born with a compass implanted in her head. She is quite able to navigate to anywhere as long as she has been there once. She never forgets the way, even if years have elapsed between visits.

I guess that's why she becomes frustrated whenever I choose to depend on my navigational device instead of simply asking her for directions. Once when we lived in Arizona, our family felt like finding some ice cream. I punched my request into my machine and it instantly delivered a destination where we could presumably acquire a frozen treat. Aimee continued to exercise patience as my device began to direct me into a residential neighborhood and away from the more commercially dense areas where one would expect to find an ice cream parlor. I was likewise determined to show her that my navigational machine knew exactly where to find ice cream. In the end, I was directed to a condo development in Scottsdale. Pulling into a private residential driveway, I turned off the engine, looked back at the kids, and instructed, "Now remember kids, this is some-body's home, so be on your best behavior." With that, we all burst out laughing. Obviously, my navigation device had no idea where the nearest ice cream parlor was. Not to leave you hanging, we did not actually knock on the door and demand ice cream. We eventually found some in a nearby commercial center.

Your strategic directives are much like the ice cream parlor in this story. They represent destinations, places where we want to take the community. However, simply articulating our priorities brings us no closer to realizing our vision. We need directions. This is the next part of the strategic planning process. If our *directives* represent destinations, strategic *initiatives* represent the directions to our destinations. Just like Rick's experience of trying to find ice cream with his family, if our initiatives are not well thought out, we will indeed find ourselves at a destination . . . just not the one that we intended. That's why a great deal of thought needs to be invested in development of the specific initiatives that you will prescribe in the plan.

A strategic initiative is still a very broad idea that needs to be implemented in order to bring about the realization of the strategic directive to which it is tied. If, for example, your strategic directive speaks to the need of improving and maintaining community aesthetics, one appropriate initiative may prescribe a greater emphasis by neighborhood code enforcement. If another directive speaks to the importance of fiscal sustainability, perhaps a relevant initiative may suggest the creation of a community fiscal readiness plan.

You will recall that in order to develop your strategic directives, you answered four very important questions. Just as your strategic directive will suggest how to sustain the good things that are happening in your community as well as address noted deficiencies, your strategic initiatives will accomplish the same thing, only with a little bit more specificity than did your directives. So let's go back to what we noted about our Community Health and Safety directive. The following table captures some of the more salient points:

Community Health and Safety	
What did the citizens say and what have we noticed?	» Uptick of crime in southern neighborhoods » Professional public safety personnel » Deteriorating appearance in southern neighborhoods » Satisfaction with downtown core appearance » Perception of slow police response times » Children do not have adequate safe walking routes to school » Low crime rate » Some dangerous intersections in town could benefit from signalization
What do we like?	» Professional and courteous police » Well-maintained downtown core » Fire educational outreach » Fairly low crime rate » Equipment appears new and modern » Deployment of emergency personnel appears adequate

Community Health and Safety	
What do we see going wrong?	» Uncertain that municipal government is maintaining emergency personnel staffing congruent with growth » Deteriorating neighborhoods becoming a hotbed for crime » Children observed walking in road right-of-way to school » Lack of adequate street lighting in many areas of the community exacerbating safety concerns
Where are the specific deficiencies?	» Code enforcement efforts inadequate, especially in southern neighborhoods » Lack of infrastructure maintenance in southern neighborhoods, i.e. sidewalks, roadways, abatement of weeds and overgrowth, etc. » Inadequate street lighting » Signalization at several dangerous intersections » Plan to maintain stasis with growth as such pertains to emergency personnel staffing

As we look at this pretty comprehensive list, let's highlight any of the items that we believe are important to reinforce and continue supporting. For this example, see the items underlined in the following table:

Community Health and Safety	
What the citizens say and what have we noticed?	» Uptick of crime in southern neighborhoods » *Professional public safety personnel* » Deteriorating appearance in southern neighborhoods » *Satisfaction with downtown core appearance* » Perception of slow police response times

Community Health and Safety	
	» Children do not have adequate safe walking routes to school » *Low crime rate* » Some dangerous intersections in town could benefit from signalization
What do we like?	» *Professional and courteous police* » *Well-maintained downtown core* » *Fire educational outreach* » *Fairly low crime rate* » *Equipment appears new and modern* » *Deployment of emergency personnel appears adequate*
What do we see going wrong?	» Uncertain that local government is maintaining emergency personnel staffing congruent with growth » Deteriorating neighborhoods becoming a hotbed for crime » Children observed walking in road right-of-way to school » Lack of adequate street lighting in many areas of the community exacerbating safety concerns
Where are the specific deficiencies?	» Code enforcement efforts inadequate, especially in southern neighborhoods » Lack of infrastructural maintenance in southern neighborhoods, i.e. sidewalks, roadways, abatement of weeds and overgrowth, etc. » Inadequate street lighting » Signalization at several dangerous intersections » Plan to maintain stasis with growth as such pertains to emergency personnel staffing

In this portion of the exercise, we may feel that our plan needs to specifically reinforce these highlighted elements, perhaps because they bear greater connectivity to other initiatives that we are going to propose. Maybe our committee fears that without such reinforcement in the strategic plan, conditions may deteriorate in these areas. There is really no end of reasons why you would want to reinforce in your plan things that are already going right. The principle here is that your plan need not only contain initiatives to address deficiencies. We are after all just as interested in continuing all the good things that happen in our community.

Now, let's highlight some of the deficiencies that we want to specifically address in the plan. See these items underlined in the following table:

Community Health and Safety	
What the citizens say and what have we noticed?	» Uptick of crime in southern neighborhoods » Professional public safety personnel » *Deteriorating appearance in southern neighborhoods* » Satisfaction with downtown core appearance » Perception of slow police response times » *Children do not have adequate safe walking routes to school* » Low crime rate » Some dangerous intersections in town could benefit from signalization

Community Health and Safety	
What do we like?	» Professional and courteous police » Well-maintained downtown core » Fire educational outreach » Fairly low crime rate » Equipment appears new and modern » Deployment of emergency personnel appears adequate
What do we see going wrong?	» Uncertain that local government is maintaining emergency personnel staffing congruent with growth » Deteriorating neighborhoods becoming a hotbed for crime » Children observed walking in road right-of-way to school.
Where are the specific deficiencies?	» *Code enforcement efforts inadequate, especially in southern neighborhoods* » *Lack of infrastructural maintenance in southern neighborhoods, i.e. sidewalks, roadways, abatement of weeds and overgrowth, etc.* » *Inadequate street lighting* » *Signalization at several dangerous intersections* » *Plan to maintain stasis with growth as such pertains to emergency personnel staffing*

Taking all of these elements together, it becomes a little clearer what our community needs to do to maintain our city as a healthy and safe place.

First, we want to maintain an adequate staffing of courteous, professional, and well-equipped emergency personnel, sufficient to meet our needs now and in the future as we continue to grow. The safety of our children is absolutely critical and we therefore need adequate sidewalks and lighting to accommodate their commute to school. Our citizens also deserve adequate street lighting and intersection signalization to keep them safe. Finally, we need to make sure that all citizens recognize their responsibility to maintain private properties as a means of deterring crime and maximizing property values. Such efforts need to include a renewed commitment on the part of the municipal government to address infrastructure deficiencies in some parts of the community.

The next thing we need to do is articulate what we stated above as single initiatives tied to our strategic directive, as follows:

STRATEGIC DIRECTIVE 1
COMMUNITY HEALTH AND SAFETY

Metro City is a healthy and safe community. As such, we work together to build and maintain neighborhoods that contribute to the quality of our community. Ours is a community that is walkable at all hours and that provides multiple and safe means of transportation. Police and fire are staffed with the most dedicated personnel and provided the finest equipment to meet the demands of our growing community.

Value Statement

In Metro City, community health and safety is foundational to quality of life. We therefore regard the investment in elements that contribute to health and safety as the paramount responsibility of citizens and their local government. We expect all community members to work together to ensure the safety of our citizens by supporting this investment and by maintaining our neighborhoods as safe and healthy places for individuals and families.

We propose accomplishing this directive through the effective implementation of the following strategic initiatives:

Initiatives

» *Develop and implement a strategic public safety/emergency personnel staffing plan.*

» *Aggressively address sidewalk deficiencies along*

designated school walking routes.

» *Revise/revisit street lighting plan and develop and implement a plan to meet deficiencies.*

» *Increase code enforcement efforts in southern portion of the community and coordinate efforts with
Police Department.*

» *Work in concert with state Department of Transportation
to develop and implement plan addressing signalization deficiencies at intersections where improvements
meet warrants.*

» *Support/fund public outreach efforts on the part of public
safety agencies.*

» *Develop and implement cement replacement and asphalt
maintenance schedule specific to southern portion of
the community.*

Do you see the power in this? The citizens of our hypothetical community have stated that they will support local government efforts to
address these deficiencies. When it comes to community health and
safety, at least for the next five years, elected officials and administrators should have little doubt in what direction they should point budget
allocations. The citizens of Metro City have made their priorities clear!
This allows us to have the discipline to say no to public safety and health
proposals that do not align with our strategic directive and the courage
to say yes to those that do. Instead of being all things to all people, can
you see how Metro City will be able to focus their finite resources on the
things that matter most?

And we're not done yet. An important part of the work you are doing for the strategic plan involves the articulation of desired outcomes.
We are not going to state these in purely quantitative terms. We will
leave that for the administrator. But we *are* going to communicate to
the elected body, "We will know that you have effectively implemented
the strategic directive if we see the following." We will then go on to

describe what we think Metro City will look like in five years in terms of community health and safety.

Perhaps we will articulate this as follows:

» *School children are provided adequate sidewalks and walking paths which are maintained clear of debris and snow.*

» *All streets are adequately lit.*

» *Intersections that have met applicable warrants have been signalized.*

» *Code enforcement has effectively worked with law enforcement in the southern portion of the community to mitigate violations. Code enforcement is visible and residents have begun to take responsibility for maintaining their properties.*

» *The capital improvement plan has adequately targeted and executed improvements to walkways and roadways in the southern portion of the community. Infrastructure in this part of our community has improved significantly.*

» *Emergency personnel are visible and engaged in the community and growth in personnel numbers has been commensurate with community growth.*

The elected body and administration now have almost everything they need, except funding perhaps, to address citizen expectations specific to community health and safety. I said "almost." During the course of data-gathering, some of the residents and stakeholders remained very general with regard to their ideas and expectations. Others got right down to the atomic level! Many of these specific ideas are very helpful to the municipal government as they begin to plan for projects during the year. While they are much too specific and narrow to include as initiatives, there is a place for them in the strategic plan. We call such a place the "Tool Box" which is generally included as an appendix at the end of the plan so as not to distract from the key priorities articulated through the directives and initiatives.

The Tool Box

Just as the name implies, the Tool Box is a congregation of various ideas which were assembled during the data gathering phase. Unlike directives and initiatives, tool box items tend to be extremely specific. For example, while many citizens may have expressed a concern with regard to general traffic circulation within your community, perhaps someone suggested "widening Elm Street from Becker to Homestead Drive." Another respondent may have chimed in with a specific idea regarding economic development with "get a _____ (full-service restaurant) on the south end of town."

Obviously, these ideas are not articulated broadly enough to enable our inclusion of this feedback as directives or initiatives. They are nonetheless important because of their potential in assisting the local government in continuing to correctly interpret the expectations of citizens. Perhaps you have done a bit of hiking before in a location where the trail is difficult to locate. Fortunately for you and other hikers, someone has marked the trail at various locations. This is usually done with a stack of rocks, perhaps signage, or something else visible enough to provide assurance to hikers that they are still on the designated trail. That's what toolbox items are for. They let us know down to a very specific level what citizens were thinking with regard to a given directive.

Now, just a few words of caution about toolbox items. First, the strategic planning committee is under no obligation to include every suggestion uttered by the mouth of a citizen in the strategic plan. "Throw the Mayor out" is not a toolbox item that should be included in the strategic plan. Once we received a comment from a survey participant who, when asked what he would *change* about the city, replied "me in it." Another spent several paragraphs expressing their frustrations with a state senator. Filtering is a necessary function of the committee. You are looking for mile marker comments and other ideas that will give the community a pathway going forward.

Second, not every toolbox idea is necessarily immediately imple-mentable. If the committee has done its job, municipal leadership will be left with a series of specific ideas associated with each directive that contributing citizens believe are not only possible but indeed the re-sponsibility of the local government to complete. From their sometimes-limited perspective, they may believe that their municipal government has the power to install signalization on a state highway or build more schools. Other citizens may have suggested the construction of a bridge over a waterway that municipal officials recognize would be astronomi-cally unaffordable. Does that mean that you exclude a relevant toolbox idea that is deemed infeasible? Perhaps not. Some make the mistake of assuming that the toolbox represents a "to do list." Again, the toolbox serves as a repository of possible projects or community improvement ideas, but it is *not* the citizens' version of the "honey-do list." Don't make the mistake of assuming that you need to complete everything articulated by your citizens. "But aren't they going to expect you to do it if you put it into your plan?" you may ask. Let's face it. There are going to be citizens who expect you to do a lot of things that are *not* in the plan. So the answer is, of course. However, for the reasonable, you can explain the purpose of the toolbox in your plan narrative, and that should suffice. Besides, even in those circumstances where you may not be able to effect the change suggested by a citizen, your local government may have an advocacy role that could expedite realization.

At this point we can imagine you saying to yourself: "What if citizens articulate a host of unaffordable priorities and all we do is increase the level of discontent by creating a plan with no funds for implementation?" This is a very fair question. Perhaps a story will illustrate.

One community that I served had a serious debt problem. Past elect-ed officials had succumbed to the siren song of an investment banker who convinced them to take on an extremely risky bond to fund infra-structure improvements that were sure to lead to increased develop-ment and tax revenues that would enable repayment of the bond. "If you build it, they will come" was the refrain. Unfortunately, the bonds were issued, the infrastructure built out, but "they" didn't come. The projections on which the bond was based seem ridiculous in hindsight, but the debt remains and the piper will have to be paid.

In this extreme example, the strategic planning exercise at first seemed like a waste of time. Why should the municipal government plan for anything when the albatross of debt would make it impossible to make meaningful investments in any of the strategic directives and initiatives? As it turned out, the strategic planning exercise served a couple of important functions:

7. **Education** – It helped educate citizens about the magnitude of the debt problem and prioritize steps that would enable the local government to eventually get out from under this tremendous burden, including things like direct negotiations with the bondholders. It also provided elected officials with the courage to pursue other revenue opportunities (tax and fee increases) for the local government because residents now understood what was at stake for their community.

8. **Focus** – The planning exercise provided needed focus for the very limited resources in this community. Because this municipality had such finite resources, the allocation of those resources in alignment with citizen priorities became even more critical. The planning process enabled staff to identify where to focus and gave them permission to let go of those things outside of the truly essential priorities of their citizens.

Did the plan also include a few likely unaffordable "wish list" kinds of items? Absolutely. Every plan we have encountered will have a few of these items. However, this provided a doorway to productive conversations about the affordability of such items and allowed citizens to feel that their local government had listened to what was important to them. And let's remember, some things that are deemed unaffordable today, could be later. At the very least, citizens expect that their local *government will investigate and possibly plan for the day when a citizen priority will be possible.*

Let's now continue with our example by adding a toolbox section to our directive "Community Health and Safety." For the purpose of continuity, we will restate our strategic directive, our value statement, our initiatives, and our expected outcomes.

STRATEGIC DIRECTIVE 1
COMMUNITY HEALTH AND SAFETY

Metro City is a healthy and safe community. As such, we work together to build and maintain neighborhoods that contribute to the quality of our community. Ours is a community that is walkable at all hours and that provides multiple and safe means of transportation. Police and fire are staffed with the most dedicated personnel and provided the finest equipment to meet the demands of our growing community.

Value Statement

In Metro City, community health and safety is foundational to quality of life. We therefore regard the investment in elements that contribute to health and safety as the paramount responsibility of citizens and their local government. We expect all community members to work together to ensure the safety of our citizens by supporting this investment and by maintaining our neighborhoods as safe and healthy places for individuals and families.

We propose accomplishing this directive through the effective implementation of the following strategic initiatives:

Initiatives

> *Develop and implement a strategic public safety/emergency personnel staffing plan.*

> *Aggressively address sidewalk deficiencies along designated school walking routes.*

> *Revise/revisit street lighting plan and develop and implement a plan to meet deficiencies.*

» *Increase code enforcement efforts in southern portion of the community. Coordinate code enforcement efforts with Police Department.*

» *Work in concert with state Department of Transportation to develop and implement plan addressing signalization deficiencies at intersections where improvements meet warrants.*

» *Support/fund public outreach efforts on the part of public safety agencies.*

» *Implement aggressive schedule of patrol car and fire apparatus replacement in order to maintain modern emergency response fleet.*

» *Develop and implement weed abatement program.*

» *Develop and implement cement replacement and asphalt maintenance schedule specific to southern portion of the community.*

Expected Outcomes

» *Emergency personnel staffing has met and maintained parity with population growth.*

» *School children are provided adequate sidewalks and walking paths which are maintained clear of debris and snow.*

» *All streets are adequately lit.*

» *Intersections that have met applicable warrants have been signalized.*

» *Code enforcement has effectively worked with law enforcement in the southern portion of the community to mitigate violations. Code enforcement is visible and residents have begun to take responsibility for maintaining their properties.*

» *The capital improvement plan has adequately targeted and executed improvements to walkways and roadways in the southern portion of the community. Infrastructure in this part of our community has improved significantly.*

» *The city has maintained a modern emergency re-sponse fleet.*

» *Emergency personnel are visible and engaged in the community.*

And now we are going to add some specific ideas that were provided by citizens relevant to this strategic directive. Keep in mind that tool box items can be placed in an appendix of your plan. In keeping with the purpose of the tool box (i.e. not a to-do list for the municipal government), our preference is to include the tool box in an appendix. Nevertheless, let's say we received the following ideas from citizens:

Tool Box Items

» *Build a new fire station in Ridge Hills area.*

» *Re-paint retaining wall at community center with graffiti resistant paint.*

» *Install a traffic signal at Hill Field Road and Garner Pass Road.*

» *Build a sidewalk for Hock Elementary along the east side of Lewis Drive.*

» *Install a street light at the end of Vickrey circle.*

» *Create sidewalk between Main Park and downtown.*

» *Enforce leash law at Barker Park.*

» *More firefighters in schools teaching CPR.*

» *Let seniors volunteer for Police Department.*

» *Build an additional high school.*

» *Increase fine for littering.*

» *Put crosswalk across Netters Avenue.*

» *Make graffiti artists clean up own mess.*

» *More cops at night.*

Now we have a completed strategic directive! You are going to want to go through this process for every one of your directives. By now, you should be able to see how this is going to require time and patience. Believe me when I tell you that your strategic planning committee is going to put in a lot of hours; but in the end, they will have experienced something that few citizens ever will, and they will bond with their community in a way that they never thought possible.

Before wrapping up a discussion of strategic directives, there is one last portion of your strategic plan that you may want to consider including once you have completed your directives. It will initially seem like we have put the cart before the horse by bringing this last element to your attention at the end of developing your strategic directives. In fact, it is generally necessary to begin the articulation of your strategic directives before focusing on what we will refer to as the "Primary Directive."

Primary Directive

For the purpose of completely explaining the concept of the primary directive, we will liberally refer to author Jim Collins' book Good to Great, mentioned previously. Actually, it wasn't until we read this book that we truly recognized the importance of a primary directive. We used to think that simply identifying and developing strategic directives was probably enough. However, the meaning and relevance of your strategic directives take on a powerful new dimension when tied to a *primary* directive.

A primary directive meanwhile is not a mission statement per se. It is a crystal-clear idea and statement of why your organization exists, why your community exists. Collins refers to this idea as a "hedgehog concept." As he puts it, the name is derived from a spiny little critter whose only defense from a hungry fox is to curl up into a ball and expose its pointy backside to the predator. While the fox darts from one side to the other and employs every maneuver that a hungry fox knows to use, the hedgehog knows to do one thing. It is focused on that one strategy, ignores any other, does it well, and emerges victorious from the vast majority of such encounters.[16]

Collins has noted through his research that successful organizations behave more like hedgehogs than they do foxes. In essence, hedgehogs focus on the essential and have the discipline to ignore everything else. Speaking of successful private sector companies, Collins says, " . . . All the good-to-great companies attained a very simple concept that they used as a frame of reference for all their decisions, and this understanding coincided with breakthrough results."[17] Collins says that great organizations have tied their strategies to a deep understanding of three essential dimensions, what Collins refers to as the three circles. These organizations have translated these three circles or dimensions into a crystal-clear idea that has guided and continues to guide all of their decision-making.

So why have we waited until this point to discuss what is aptly regarded as a foundational understanding of why your local government exists? The answer is so simple it may startle you. For most communities, until they engage in a strategic planning process and thoroughly develop strategic directives and initiatives, it is highly likely that their understanding of their own community is not deep enough to be able to answer three basic questions:

1. *What can we as a community be the best in the world at?*

2. *What drives our resource engine?*

3. *What are we deeply passionate about?*

These are the three dimensions that Collins describes in his book. At the intersection of these three answers we find our hedgehog concept, or as we presented in this book, a primary directive. Allow us to touch on each one of these as they relate to the business of communities.

---

[16] Jim Collins, *Good to Great* (New York: HarperBusiness, 2001), 90.

[17] Collins, 95.

First, what can our community be the best in the world at? Please understand at this point that there is a distinct difference between an understanding of what we can be the best in the world at and a goal *to be* the best in the world at something. We are not asking you to set world domination as a goal. We are asking you to understand at a very deep level what you think your community could be the best at. Again, most communities don't completely understand the answer to this question until they've taken the time to go through a strategic planning process. Such an exercise reveals not only what we can be the best in the world at, but it also allows us to clearly see and embrace what we *cannot* be the best at. **I recall one community with which I worked desiring to become a tourism mecca. The only problem was that there was scarcely anything in town that was powerful enough to draw that level of attention. What compounded this town's problem was the fact that it sat adjacent to one of the "biggest and baddest" tourism venues in the world. It was going to have to find its own niche. The topper was the fact that citizens during the strategic planning process didn't see their community as a tourism venue at all, and they would have likely been unhappy with any effort on the part of the city to pursue such a direction.**

Second, what drives our resource engine? In other words, what is it that we do or can do that perpetuates our ability to realize our primary directive? Obviously, if a private sector company does not make a profit, it's not too long before that company becomes extinct. However, things are a bit different in the public sector. Money does not drive our engine. You may say that without money even local governments will become extinct. That's true, but in the public sector, bringing money into local government coffers is no more the purpose of that government than eating is the purpose of life. A municipal government could have coffers overflowing with tax revenue, and still be completely impotent with regard to fulfilling its primary directive. Money in fact, where such applies to the public sector, is a hygiene factor. Money doesn't enable us to fulfill our mission, but the absence of it can certainly hamper our best efforts.

The answer is *trust*. All municipalities run on trust. As described earlier, trust is the intersectional byproduct of trustworthiness and competency. One of the greatest benefits of a strategic planning initiative is that you demonstrate both qualities to your citizens as you engage in this exercise. To reiterate, when you extend yourself to the community, invite their participation in planning their community's future, and then go about competently and effectively implementing your plan, you generate *trust*. Community trust usually translates into a willingness to continue to *en*trust resources to local government so that they can continue to demonstrate their trustworthiness and competency, which results in greater trust, which results in continued resources, and round and round the wheel spins. To see how this works in action, let's describe a situation in one of the communities with which we worked.

It had been 25 years since the community had been presented with a possible property tax increase. Unfortunately, other revenue sources had not grown sufficiently to maintain parity with explosive residential growth. Previous elected bodies had been borrowing from fund reserves in an effort to stave off the consideration of an unpopular property tax increase. We call this political maneuver "kicking the can." It characterizes what some elected officials do when they don't want to make an unpopular decision. They simply "kick the can" or move the decision to a future elected body.

In this particular community, they were receiving warning letters from financial rating companies noting that their fund reserves were dangerously low. In order to maintain their favorable bond rating, the municipality would need to show its earnestness in maintaining a solvent financial situation. Meanwhile, financial projections showed very little hope of the local government avoiding insolvency unless it drastically cut expenses and/or increased property taxes. The problem with slashing costs was that more than three quarters of every dollar spent by the municipal government was invested in core public safety programs. Simply laying off an administrative employee or two or cutting positions in the planning department wasn't going to affect their situation. A long-time employee was very helpful in describing the blood and carnage that had followed the last proposal to raise property taxes. Hundreds of angry residents turned out to the hearing. This was not only a rake in the grass, it was a chainsaw!

Fortunately, that municipality had completed a community-based strategic planning exercise with their citizens. They had stated that public safety was their number one priority. Other directives included proactive maintenance of infrastructure, fiscal sustainability, and improved community aesthetics. None of these were going to be remotely possible without changing the trajectory of their revenue. By staff's calculations, they were set to run out of money by mid-decade without a property tax increase. State law required that they pass through many public notification processes and steps before ultimately holding a public hearing at which the tax increase would be established. Although the elected officials' knees were shaky, the strategic plan supported this type of action.

When the day came for the public hearing, three citizens showed up—a gentleman who spoke against the tax increase, a gentleman who spoke in favor of the tax increase, and the same eccentric, elderly lady who attended all meetings. Where were the torches? Where were the pitchforks? Citizens protested the property tax increase proposed only a few years earlier, in much more prosperous times mind you, because they didn't *trust* their local government. Few showed up this time because trust had increased. As the municipal manager meandered through the community in the following weeks, dozens of citizens told him that they thought it was about time that the city adjust the property tax. Most said that they understood this time what the city was going to do with it, and that was good enough for them.

Third, what are we deeply passionate about? Most public servants chose the vocation that they did because they are passionate about helping people, about making life better. Now that may change over the course of their career, but for most, it's where they started. City Hall tends to be staffed with people who are engaged in what they believe to be a good cause. They love their community and they are passionate about quality of life.

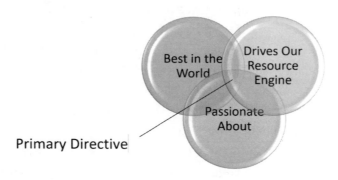

There are likely some reading this who will decide that their current organizational mission statement suits them fine and that there is no need to reinvent the wheel with a primary directive, and that's okay. The principle that I'm describing here involves taking a central concept and making that the hub of the wheel to which your strategic directives are tied. In fact, every strategic directive you develop should support your central mission.

In one of the communities we assisted, they illustrated this relationship as follows:

This community's primary directive, as it was determined by the strategic planning committee, in concert with staff and elected officials, remains to this day:

"To provide our citizens with the opportunity to live and enjoy an exceptional quality of life."

It doesn't get any simpler than that. And it's something that can sit in the center of every one of their strategic directives. In other words, every directive and every initiative supports this central concept. If you have a mission statement, meanwhile, that you want to use, ask yourself if it accomplishes what we've described here. Is it a guide to your decision-making? Does it govern which programs you support? Does it serve as a gauge to help you determine whether you are effective? If it does, that is probably a pretty good primary directive. As one hint, most primary directives for municipal governments will include some reference to quality of life. How you articulate that for your community is what makes you unique.

Just where to place your primary directive in your plan is up to you and your committee, but we generally suggest placing it at the beginning. We have found it effective if you also describe how you arrived at your central mission statement or primary directive.

Additional Elements of the Plan, Final Touches

We have discussed all of the primary elements that need to go into your strategic plan. However, we want to make sure that you understand that there are some less obvious elements that you can add to your plan to dress it up and make it flow better.

First, we always suggest putting together a cover to your plan that is clean, professional, and uncluttered. It should carry a simple title such as "Community Strategic Plan for the City/County/Town/Borough of _____" or other similar heading. You may want to include a few images in the form of photos that perhaps tie back to the strategic directives. This may seem obvious to many of you, but do everything you can to use photos from your specific community. Stock photos can be cute, but they are no substitute for actual photos from your community. In terms of the use of other graphic elements such as logos, it's best to place the local government's official logo on the cover. It is more appropriate, if you so desire, to utilize the strategic planning logo and slogan in the body of the plan or at the conclusion. Finally, please make sure that your cover provides the effective dates of the strategic plan. Remember that this is a five-year plan, so annual dates that reflect this would be appropriate.

Next, insert a title page that provides a guide to the various sections of the plan. A nice introductory letter from the chief elected official is also a nice touch. He or she should explain why the community thought it necessary to engage in a strategic planning process, offer some explanation of how the community will benefit from such a plan, and express appreciation to the committee, staff, and citizens that made the plan possible. Many municipalities prefer, before getting into the body of the report, to provide a short description of the history and character of their community. It may even be appropriate to share some statistics or a short demographic profile. We have also found it effective to share a brief synopsis of the strategic planning project and methodologies used in the process. This should be done in a way that makes it clear that this was an official initiative, guided by a citizen volunteer committee. At the conclusion of the report, be sure to include a short "Special Thanks" that recognizes the support of the elected officials, staff, and committee, as well as the contributions of citizens and other stakeholders.

When you have completed the plan, you are probably going to be left with 20–30 pages (although only about 5–10 pages of the plan will contain the meat of the directives and initiatives). This is a sizable document to simply print in bulk and distribute among your citizens. Many communities therefore condense the strategic plan into a citizen brochure that can be easily replicated and distributed. We will talk more about communicating the plan to citizens in the next chapter. Meanwhile, you now have a plan that is ready and worthy to take to your elected body and citizens!

CONCLUSION

With strategic directives identified, the central purpose of the strategic planning committee is to begin the composition of the strategic plan. If strategic directives represent the destination of our plan, the composition of other plan elements, such as strategic initiatives, represent the directions that are going to take us to our destination. The strategic planning committee can begin the composition of strategic initiatives by closely examining both what they have observed as being appreciated by the community and what is currently deficient. Initiatives propose action on the part of the local government to both reinforce the positive things that are occurring as well as fill the holes where deficiencies have become evident. As you and your committee compose these action items, you will want to remain fairly broad in the way that you articulate them. Greater clarity can be provided by the committee by including a section following each grouping of initiatives that describes desired outcomes. Meanwhile, some ideas generated by planning participants during the process may be so specific that they are not usable as directives or initiatives. They may nevertheless be helpful and relevant in the context of one of the broader directives. We would generally place these specific action items into a section that we call our "Tool Box." A final section that any strategic planning committee may want to consider involves the development and articulation of a primary directive. A primary directive is a clear and concise statement of why the organization exists. It also serves as the hub of the plan to which all directives are tied. In other words, all strategic directives support the primary directive. In developing the primary directive, the committee will want to consider three important questions: 1) What can we be the best in the world at? 2) What drives our resource engine? and 3) What are we deeply passionate about? There are several other elements that should be part of the final composition of your plan.

These include a cover, title page, mayor's message, a description of the process, and special thanks. While the full plan can be expected to be sizable, many jurisdictions find it helpful to print smaller citizen brochures that focus on the articulation of key strategic directives.

TAKEAWAYS

» *If our directives represent destinations, strategic initiatives represent the directions to our destinations.*

» *Just as your strategic directives will suggest how to sustain the good things that are happening in your community as well as address noted deficiencies, your strategic initiatives will accomplish the same thing, only with a little bit more specificity than did your directives.*

» *An important part of the work you are doing with regard to the strategic plan involves the articulation of desired outcomes.*

» *During the course of data gathering, some of the residents and stakeholders remained very general with regard to their ideas and expectations. Others got right down to the atomic level! Many of these very specific ideas are very helpful to the municipal government as they begin to plan for specific projects during the year. While they are much too specific and narrow to include as initiatives, there is a place for them in the strategic plan. We call such a place the "Tool Box."*

» *Not every tool box idea is necessarily immediately implementable. The tool box serves certainly as a repository of possible projects or community improvement ideas, but it is not the citizens' version of the "honey-do list." Don't make the mistake of assuming that you need to complete everything articulated by your citizens.*

» *Great organizations have tied their strategies to a primary directive that incorporates a deep understanding of three essential dimensions. These dimensions are characterized by the answers to three corresponding questions: 1) What can we be the best in the world at? 2) What drives our resource engine? and 3) What are we deeply passionate about? Lying at the intersection of these three dimensions is the primary directive.*

8

PUTTING THE PLAN INTO ACTION

"An organization's ability to learn and translate that learning into
action rapidly is the ultimate competitive advantage."
— Jack Welch

When I was a kid, I and my friends used to play football in the middle of the street that ran in front of our homes. We would use the curbs as the sidelines and the telephone poles as touchdown markers. Just like authentic football, we would huddle before each snap of the ball to plan our short-term strategy. Usually, the quarterback was in charge of drawing a series of patterns and assignments with his finger on the palm of his hand. "Rick, you're going to go out 10 steps and cut to your right. Mike, you run straight out in front of me five steps then turn around. Tom, you're going to line up on my left, go straight out about 30 feet, and slant right." With the plan explained and assignments understood, the quarterback would confidently take the ball in hand and with a "hut, hut . . . hike!" he'd snap the ball to himself, fade backwards like Joe Namath, and prepare to deliver the ball just as planned. Unfortunately, when the

ball was snapped, most of us abandoned our assignments as if we had never huddled and ran the distance of the "field" looking for the Hail Mary pass. Disaster was usually the byproduct.

The moral of the story is that it really doesn't matter how good your plan is if you don't put it into action correctly. And while it has been said many times that no plan survives contact with the enemy, yours certainly must. Your plan represents, as closely as anything else in the community, your citizens' united declaration of what they expect from their local government. It would be a little more than just a sin to simply take the work that you and the committee have done, place it on a shelf, and walk away. We'll spend this chapter discussing how to translate that new strategic plan into action and tangible deliverables. Most of what we will share is directed at two primary audiences, the strategic planning committee and elected and appointed leadership.

Begin at the Beginning

Just as it was critically important that your local governing body establish the strategic planning project and committee by official decree, so it is equally important that the elected body formally adopt the strategic plan by resolution. This will require that your committee work with administration to assemble a presentation at a public gathering, such as a regularly scheduled meeting of the elected body. Make sure that each elected official has had time to review the entire plan a few weeks before they are to consider adoption. You may want to make sure that your local reporter has had a preview of the plan and that you have designated someone from municipal staff, elected officials or your committee to interface with the reporter to clarify any issues and answer his/her questions. If you have done your work correctly, the content of the plan will surprise very few. Remember that we emphasize the importance of keeping your elected officials in the loop during the process in a very public way. In addition, you have utilized your municipal website and perhaps even social media to ensure that the press and citizens are also kept up-to-date. The presentation to the elected body will therefore feel more like a celebration than an unveiling.

However, it's even more than a celebration. Aside from the "high fives" associated with completing the plan, the official adoption and ratification of the plan brings a great deal of legitimacy to the plan itself. While this is not enough to ensure that the plan will be put into action, it's an important first step. Citizens, staff, administration, stakeholders, and the elected body will all know that your community means business.

After all that you have been through in the preceding months, it is difficult to comprehend how anyone could not know about your strategic plan. Even with all of the workshops, open houses, and other events you have hosted; after the numerous newspaper articles, website posts, tweets, Facebook messages, etc., it is always surprising how few people are really acquainted with the reality that their local government now has a citizen-based strategic plan. Actually, as facilitators of this process, our experience is that by the end of the process and adoption of the plan, a sizeable number of your citizens will know little about it. You may be wondering following my last assertion, "Why would we call this the citizens' plan if so many of our citizens don't know about it?" And that's a very fair question. The answer may seem a bit harsh, but we all know that there are folks who live in your community who, because of a variety of factors, are going to remain disengaged. The fact is, if you have executed the process correctly, the plan will generally represent the will of the citizens who *care* about your community, people who take the initiative and expend the energy to participate in the planning process.

The question remains, which this chapter attempts to address, how do you get everybody else on board?

Realizing that you are never going to get *everybody* on board, you need to make as many people as possible aware of the plan's existence and its contents. This is also an opportunity to acquaint your citizens with the strategic planning process, recognize those committee members who spent so much of their time and energy on developing the plan, and generally explain how the plan is going to be used in the future to make resource allocation decisions (we will cover this important topic a little later). As you did at the beginning of the data gathering phase, tapping into the resources of your stakeholder group is the most effective way of communicating with citizens. So as not to repeat, we recommend that you briefly review that part of the book where we discussed working with stakeholder groups. Beyond this, it is advisable to create an electronic version of the plan that can be posted on your website and a hard copy (paper) citizens' brochure that can be placed at the utility counter or other appropriate places where citizens will have access to it. Since the intention is for people to actually read the plan, we recommend that you condense your full plan into a short version that highlights the key elements of the plan, i.e. the directives and initiatives. You may also want to place the mayor's introductory letter or statement in this type of brochure. And while we're at it, make sure that the chamber has enough of these to place inside their welcome packets or at the chamber office.

Making the Plan Relevant

At this point, we are going to assume that you have successfully ratified your plan and that you have effectively communicated its existence and contents to your citizens and stakeholders. Even as you are in the process of doing so, it is critically important that you begin putting the plan into action. After all, simply telling people that you have a plan is not going to be enough. The ultimate purpose of the strategic plan is to provide citizen-based direction connected to priorities that are most important to the community and to prescribe a pathway to realizing these directives.

If you've been around local government for any amount of time, you quickly learn that the primary policy statement from year to year is the annual budget. The supremacy of this document in communicating the year's spending priorities is unmatched. Therefore, the most effective way to make your strategic plan relevant and effective is to link it to the budgetary process. Upon adoption of the strategic plan, the elected body should direct administration to develop methods for ensuring that future resource allocations are made in accordance with the directives articulated in the plan. That's very easy to say, but not so easy to do.

One of the difficulties of translating the strategic plan into a budget reality is the fact that many functions of local government may enjoy little to no connectivity with the tenets of the strategic plan. For example, services provided by administration and the legal department, not to mention human resources, may support efforts that will be needed in order to realize the directives of the strategic plan, but it may be difficult to connect the efforts of the clerk's office in filling government information requests to one of the strategic directives. These day-to-day functions are essential, but their relevance to the plan may be vague. The strategic plan is not designed to capture every activity of the city. It is designed to draw attention and focus to the priorities that citizens have identified as *most* important. This is the same in a corporate environment. A strategic plan is not intended to encompass the full scope of a company's operations. Many corporate planning endeavors place things into the two broad categories (1) Business as Usual or BAU and (2) Strategic. A strategic plan is intended to ensure that everyone knows where the focus needs to be for strategic endeavors and that resources are allocated accordingly. For a municipal government, the goal is to ensure that those programs and services that *do* support and further the directives of the plan are identified and that resources are appropriated accordingly. It is not necessary or even desirable to include all BAU items in your strategic plan.

When I was a younger municipal manager, one of the techniques that I used to ensure that we were giving due consideration to the strategic plan on an annual basis was to help the elected body use our strategic plan to create their annual goals. In fact, the very first thing that I would place in front of our elected officials as we began deliberations at our annual retreat was our strategic plan. Additionally, I would invite our strategic planning chair to lead the discussion regarding

how effective we had been in the last 12 months with regard to plan implementation. In order to facilitate this discussion, I would provide the chair with outcome measures that I and my staff had assembled. We would meet with the chair a few weeks before the retreat so that he or she knew exactly where we were in terms of meeting the intentions of the strategic directives. This was a great exercise for us as well. Such an experience allowed us to refocus and truly evaluate the effectiveness of some of the things that we were doing. However, at the retreat, we wanted the elected body to create their goals for the upcoming year with the strategic directives in mind. The strategic initiatives in the plan certainly give the elected body a head start, but it is essential that each one of the goals be tied to one or more of the strategic directives.

Once the goals have been articulated by the elected body, administration can work with the departments to compose a business plan for the upcoming year. The technique that I usually applied involved a staff retreat approximately three weeks after the annual planning retreat. It was during this time that I was able to strategize with our department heads as to what specific steps needed to be taken in order to realize the goals of the elected body. Because the goals were based on the strategic plan, we had every confidence in what we were doing in terms of furthering the plan's objectives.

With the goals front and center, we could begin putting the meat on the bones, as it were. This was a great time to refer to the tool box in our plan and pull from it any specific ideas that we had not addressed already. The business plan, once completed, was presented to the elected body, along with the goals and initiatives that they had articulated at their retreat. It's not necessarily critical that the elected body adopt the business plan by resolution or any official way, but it is imperative that administration get a firm and decisive signal from the elected body that the business plan indeed represents their consensus.

The relevance of the strategic plan is established by linking the plan's directives and initiatives to council goals. The goals then serve as the basis of the staff's business plan and ultimately of the budget itself.

The above diagram illustrates the connectivity of the strategic planning process, shown in the first three levels of the pyramid, to the formation of council goals and ultimately to the budget itself. The business plan is intended to take each one of the council goals, show its connection to the strategic plan, and detail not only the steps that are proposed to be taken in the coming fiscal year, but also describe what resources will be needed to achieve the goals. It's also an opportunity to develop outcome measures that will help indicate during and at the end of the fiscal year how effective the municipal government has been in realizing the goals articulated by the elected body. The business plan can then be used by each department as the basis of their individual budgets. It would be cumbersome to review every step associated with the composition of a municipal business plan, but we have provided an example of such a business plan in the appendix of this book. However, even *that* is not going to help a great deal unless we spend a little bit of time here discussing outcome measures.

A lot of attention has been placed recently on outcome-based budgeting in the municipal management profession. This is a concept associated with Steven R. Covey's counsel to "begin with the end in mind."[18]

---

[18] Steven R. Covey, *The 7 Habits of Highly Effective People* (New York: Simon & Schuster, 1989).

One begins the budgeting process by considering those programs, services, and initiatives that have the greatest relevancy to what you want to have happen in your community during the next year.

You will remember that part of the strategic plan composition includes an articulation of desired outcomes or results. These are different from outcome measures. The business plan is going to need to articulate the outcome measures that will be used throughout the year to demonstrate that the plan has been put effectively into action. However, before going on, it is important to describe exactly what we mean by "outcome measures." In order to accomplish this, we touch on three concepts that are commonly misused and misapplied.

These are:

>> *Inputs*

>> *Outputs*

>> *Outcomes*

An *input* is any activity or resource that we employ to engage in a specific endeavor. For example, if we were engaged in making origami animals, paper would certainly be an input. If the municipal government is engaged in traffic enforcement, an appropriate input would be patrol hours. In our origami example, the *output* associated with our input would logically be a delicately folded paper animal. Using our traffic enforcement example, the output or result of our patrol hours could be "traffic citations." However, both of these examples fail to describe *outcomes*.

Paper in and of itself is very useful, and the origami animal represents someone's idea of paper's best use at a given point in time. However, an outcome considers the purpose or intention of the activity. In our example, if the origami animal was to be given to a child, the child's satisfaction and happiness with the animal describes a logical and indeed optimal outcome. Let's look at our traffic enforcement example. Any number of inputs can be applied to traffic enforcement, including not only patrol hours, but the number of personnel assigned to traffic enforcement, the number of patrol cars or motorcycles used in traffic enforcement, etc. The outputs associated with traffic enforcement can be citations, traffic stops, general visibility, etc. However, when you consider the purpose of traffic enforcement, you arrive at a clearer picture of what the outcome or outcomes should be. Right about now, if you are a tad bit skeptical of municipal traffic enforcement, you may be saying, "Yeah, I know exactly what the outcome is . . . more money for local government." You may be right. It's the furthest thing from our intentions to debate that issue here. However, for the sake of our discussion, a logical outcome associated with the traffic enforcement program would be "reduced accident-related injuries." Now that's an outcome! There may also be other outcomes that a community is hoping for in their traffic enforcement program such as reduced crime (outcome) through greater law enforcement visibility (output). You see, *an outcome is something that affects lives.* That's what you want to be measuring! Unfortunately, many local governments spend considerable energy and time measuring things that don't matter to a whole lot of people. This creates only the illusion of thriftiness and efficiency.

We are frequently asked how many outcome measures should be assigned to each goal. This certainly depends on the goal, but we have observed the tendency on the part of goal stewards and departments to assign too many outcome measures. Generally speaking, if you have not been accustomed to assigning outcome measures to your annual goals, try not to exceed three or four well-constructed measures. On the other end of the spectrum, there are goals that could emerge from your elected body to which it is difficult to attach any meaningful outcome measures. While such circumstances could indicate that the goal itself was not terribly well-thought-out, staff is nonetheless left with the responsibility to not only implement those measures necessary to realize the goal, but also provide some measure of success or failure. Our experience is that there are no goals to which we cannot assign outcome measures. Our success in doing so may simply require more thought as we consider the true intent of the goal in question. An example will help to illustrate.

Our council had established a goal of "greater citizen engagement." Now that can mean a lot of things to a lot of people. Further probing with our elected officials gave us the direct impression that they wanted to improve the "sense of community." They wanted the general relationship between citizens and local government to become closer. They wanted citizens to feel a sense of ownership in local government. During our department director retreat, regardless of what we had learned from the council, there remained a cloud of ambiguity in how we would measure citizen engagement. We started by describing, given what the council had provided in terms of their intentions, what citizen engagement looked like. We ultimately determined that citizen engagement looked like citizens who volunteer, citizens who vote, citizens who enroll in training experiences sponsored by their local government, and citizens who attend and enjoy our events and celebrations. All of these description criteria allowed us to begin crafting outcome measures connected to "greater citizen engagement."

There are really two keys to remember here. First, it's not so important how many outcome measures you've assigned to each goal as long as the measures describe whether the goal has been successfully implemented. Second, there is always an outcome measure that can be assigned to a goal. Discovering it may take a little extra thought.

Taking the Plan to the Budget

By the time you've gone through the exercise of composing your business plan, we have little doubt that your department directors are not only highly cognizant of what the strategic plan prescribes, but they also likely have a great idea of what is going to be needed in order to realize the goals. Backing up to our previous discussion, we find it helpful to assign a department head or two to each council goal to serve as "goal stewards." Theirs is the responsibility to periodically report progress to the municipal manager with regard to the realization of a specific goal left in their care. They also have the responsibility of ensuring that outcome measures were being appropriately applied and actually "measured." Nevertheless, it is unlikely that any of your department heads, by themselves, are going to cause the death of your strategic plan or business plan. **To explain what we mean, allow me to share an experience that I had growing up.**

Each year, my father grew a garden. This wasn't a backyard variety garden. This was a one-acre monster! Every year we would set out 300 tomato plants, 250 bell pepper plants, a couple hundred squash plants, pumpkins, cucumbers, you name it. I actually grew up wondering why people had to buy their produce in a grocery store. That activity was completely foreign to me. Dad made sure that I worked with him every Saturday during the summer, and most commonly, I was assigned to till the soil at the beginning of the season and water the plants as they grew. I soon learned how important it was that I perform my tilling responsibilities correctly so as to set the stage for successful watering. You see, if my rows were crooked, water wouldn't make it to the end of the row, and I would have to walk each row with a very heavy, industrial grade hose and individually water the plants on that row. Work was so much easier if I simply made sure that my rows were straight to begin with.

Now what the heck does this have to do with strategic planning? Well, after two decades of managing cities, I have found that there is very little that you cannot effectively communicate to your department heads. Generally speaking, these are very professional individuals who have worked very hard to get to where they are; and they are typically eager to implement the directions of the municipal manager. However, it is equally critical that *they* communicate effectively with *their* subordinates. If the vision and the plan are not getting "to the end of the row," whose problem is it? Answer—it's the municipal administrator's. That's why it's critically important that each employee receives a copy of the adopted strategic plan, as well as the year's business plan. It is also critical that your department heads remain engaged with the budget team and *their* managers during the budget process.

The budget process itself is most aptly compared to a battle, hopefully not because of fighting and contention, but for another reason altogether. Like a battle, the scene begins quite organized. All of the soldiers are marshaled in the appropriate ranks, there are banners aflutter, and the general sits atop his white steed waiting to draw his saber and order the advance. We compare this scene to the feeling usually enjoyed at the end of the annual planning retreat and ultimately the staff retreat. We are always so proud of the business plan and have every confidence that our community is about to enjoy a truly magnificent year. Then the municipal manager draws his saber and yells, "Forward!" That's when chaos ensues.

Despite everyone's best intentions, departments are hit by a plethora of budget requests that may or may not have any relevancy to the goals of the elected body, much less the strategic plan. This situation is reminiscent of the clash of armies on the battlefield. What began as an orderly process has now devolved into pure chaos. **I recall one year receiving over $120 million worth of new requests from departments, when my entire operating budget was a little more than $50 million! I used to think to myself, "What are they thinking?" That's when it struck me. The water wasn't getting to the end of the row! I needed to figure out a way to filter out the irrelevant requests. I needed to straighten my rows.**

Straightening my rows was not going to be easy. The organization was very accustomed to the annual chaos associated with budget requests. Prior to my coming to the city, it was left to the municipal manager to take millions of dollars of requests and redline the ones that the manager thought unnecessary or unaffordable; and these requests could be submitted with great detail. During my first year, I was obliged to determine whether we were going to fund an "XJ11

PRV with extender platform" or a "CBC 18 Inch jack attachment." I had every impression that my department heads knew what the plan was, but obviously our middle managers and staff did not. Meanwhile, there was no system in place that effectively allowed the department heads and managers to filter budget requests. I needed to come up with a methodology. I did two things that I now recommend to you.

First, every municipality has a base budget. The base budget considers those programs and services that are going to need to be funded next year, with or without a strategic plan. Regardless of the plan, bond payments need to be made, office supplies and equipment need to be acquired, and utilities need to be paid. Most of our personnel costs will also form part of our base budget. However, when it came to new requests, I required that they be itemized on something that we called "green sheets." Now that wasn't new. The organization was using green sheets before I came on board. What was new is this . . . I reformatted the green sheets to include a table that itemized each one of the council goals. In order for any item to receive budgetary consideration, the requestor needed to articulate the relevancy of his or her request to one or more tenets of the business plan. This at least allowed us a starting point.

I did ask each one of my department heads to develop a list of new items that they believed tied most closely to our strategic directives and the council goals, and I wasn't done yet. My assistant manager would then preside over a meeting with department heads to prioritize each one of the new spending requests. Even with a strategic plan and a well-crafted business plan, you are always going to have more needs than resources unless you are a truly fortunate community. Again, if you're like the rest of us, there are very relevant and needed things that you're simply not going to be able to fund in any given year. I believe they call this situation . . . let's see, oh yes . . . Life! Get used to it. It's a world of scarcity. However, since you have a business plan that clearly articulates a pathway toward council goal realization, and since you have asked departments to prioritize their requests in alignment with this plan, the manager or administrator is now left with a manageable list from which he or she can now begin to work. And as I said, there are things that simply are going to be left unfunded, regardless of their worthiness. That leaves you a beginning list from which to work next year; or if opportunity presents itself this year, you can propose funding projects or initiatives that were excluded initially.

Most often when I explain this process of getting the department directors involved in filtering budget requests, I usually receive the question, "That all sounds fine, but don't the department directors simply fight for their own requests?" When I first instituted this process, I have to admit that I worried about that. However, with a carefully developed business plan that the department heads have helped to create and clear connectivity between that plan, council goals, and the strategic plan, you may be surprised. Your department heads are bright people. What often causes them to simply focus on their own departmental budget requests is the fact that their departmental needs are closest at hand and best understood. Provide them with visibility to what is going on in the rest of the organization, and they will very often reach the right conclusions. You need to trust people to do the right things. I did, and I was not disappointed. No one needed to tell the parks director how important it was that we acquire a new ambulance. Likewise, the police chief realized how important it was that we replace those 25-year-old irrigation pumps at our primary park. There was a little tugging here and there; but in the end, they behaved like champions—champions of the community's cause that is. Take a leap and trust your people to do the right things.

Reporting Progress and the Continued Role of the SPAC

As a strategic planning committee, your important role is far from concluded simply because the plan has been adopted and hopefully implemented by the municipal government. In establishing your responsibilities at the beginning of the process, yours should have been a five-year commission. Remember, it is likely that you will be needed along the way and in the years to come to continue clarifying the intentions and expectations of your citizens. This doesn't mean that you have to attend every meeting of the elected body and very audibly clear your throat every time you think an elected official is doing something that doesn't align with the strategic plan. However, there is a role for the SPAC after plan adoption.

Our recommendation is that the strategic planning committee have an opportunity to meet quarterly and no less than twice a year to review progress in terms of plan implementation. This is an appropriate time for administration to share outcome measures. It's also an excellent time to calendar a strategic planning committee report to the elected body. We recommend doing this annually, as part of your goal-setting retreat. You may determine to make the report in a regularly scheduled meeting of the elected body. However you do it, do it. Without regularly returning to the elected body and reporting progress, the plan will be soon forgotten and it is likely that your community will lapse into their default mode of doing things the way they've always been done. This is human nature. That's why reporting is such a critical part of effective plan implementation.

Obviously, a report to the elected body should include a short PowerPoint or other such presentation that reintroduces the strategic directives and initiatives. It's also an excellent opportunity to review desired outcomes. This presentation is most appropriately given by the strategic planning committee chair. Ample time should be provided to administration as a follow-up to provide specific outcome measure data. The presentation should conclude with the committee chair providing the committee's opinion regarding plan implementation. Essentially, we are asking whether the committee believes that the community is on track to realizing the strategic directives.

Remember that even if your public meetings are televised or streamed over the internet, relatively few of your citizens are likely tuning in or attending in person and will therefore not be privy to the information shared in your report. That is why it is important that the strategic plan annual report be placed on the municipal website for access and produced in hard copy for distribution at government offices. There are many very affordable software tools that can be plugged into your website and allow for more consistent communication of current progress relative to key elements of the strategic plan. It's best to avoid text-based reports and instead use data visualization tools that make it easier for people to quickly evaluate progress.

You may also want to work with your local reporter to create a story that summarizes the progress the community has made since plan adoption. The use of other media, especially those associated with stakeholder groups that you originally included in the process, is also advised. The goal is to ensure that as many citizens as possible in your community not only know about the existence of the strategic plan, but also know that the local government is doing something about implementing it. If you utilized a citizen survey as part of your outreach, you can consider allowing survey respondents to answer a final optional question at the end of the survey where they provide their e-mail address if they would like to receive updates about the plan. This e-mail list can be a great way of updating your most involved citizens on progress and will help build trust. It's critically important that citizens understand *how* their life is better because of the plan.

The process of reporting, meanwhile, should continue annually during the life span of the plan. We began this book by describing an appropriate period of five years. At the risk of beating a dead horse, a plan that covers any longer span usually becomes irrelevant before its time. This is especially true in the 21st century, where things change on a dime and the world has the tendency to spin two or three times in any given year. Regardless, near the end of this five-year period, the strategic planning committee will need to re-mobilize to begin the composition of the next plan.

We are often asked how long it takes to refresh a community-based strategic plan. The answer is simple: Just about as long as the first time you composed it. This is somewhat discouraging to a lot of people. The last thing anyone wants to do is have to create the wheel every five years. However, you'll find that in subsequent strategic planning cycles, your knowledge base associated with how to apply the methodologies, analyze the data, and compose the plan has been greatly expanded. It's not that the process gets any easier. It's just that your capacity to conduct the process and produce the plan become enhanced.

Meanwhile, there are going to be some of your committee members who for one reason or another have had to drop out during the half-decade lifecycle of the plan. You may even find yourself with a new chair. As vacancies present themselves on the strategic planning committee, make sure that you return to the elected body for new member appointments. It is incredibly important that you maintain the legitimacy of the strategic planning committee. As you already know how much time it took you to produce your first plan, leave yourself that amount of time in the planning process prior to the expiration of your current plan. We generally recommend mobilizing the planning process anywhere from a year to a year and three months before the end of the current plan period. Just as before, you are not only going to need the consent of the elected body for the appointment of every member of your committee, but you are also going to need ratification of the process.

CONCLUSION

One of the last steps to the strategic planning process involves its official adoption by the governing body. Just as your elected officials brought legitimacy to the process, the plan's adoption by the elected body brings legitimacy to the plan and helps ensure that it will be used. It is also important that the municipal government make every effort to maximize the number of citizens who know about the plan and are familiar with progress in implementing it. The most powerful way to implement the plan is to link it to the budget process. This is most effectively done if the elected body uses the plan to set annual goals. Administration should use these goals to compose its annual business plan. The business plan not only shows the relevancy of goals to the strategic plan, but also allows the identification of outcome measures. In prescribing outcome measures, it is critical that you measure true outcomes, or things that matter to people. Resist the tendency to measure things that are easy to measure, like inputs. The business plan itself is only as effective and relevant as your success in getting department heads, middle managers, and line staff to implement it. Finally, while a five-year strategic plan can represent a power tool for establishing your community's future, it may become obsolete before its time if it attempts to cover a larger span of time. Make sure that your SPAC remains engaged on a regular basis in gauging and reporting plan implementation progress to the governing body through the life span of the plan. The committee should also plan to mobilize well before the end of the plan's five-year life span. The process associated with remaking your strategic plan is basically the same as the first time you created the plan. However, because you've been through the process before, you can expect that your understanding of that process and your capacity to efficiently carry it out will be greatly expanded.

TAKEAWAYS

> » *It is critically important that you make citizens aware of the strategic plan's existence and its contents. The goal is to ensure that as many citizens in your community not only know about the existence of the strategic plan, but also know that progress is being made in implementing it. It's also critically important that citizens understand how their life is better because of the plan.*

> » *The ultimate budgetary objective of strategic planning is to*

ensure that those programs and services that do support and further the directives of the plan are identified and that resources are appropriated accordingly. An important way you can ensure that you are giving due consideration to the strategic plan on an annual basis is to help the elected body use the strategic plan to create their annual goals.

» *The strategic initiatives in the plan provide the elected body a head start in creating their own goals for the year, but it is essential that each one of the goals be tied to one or more of the strategic directives. Once the goals have been articulated by the elected body, administration can work with the departments to compose a business plan for the upcoming year.*

» *The business plan is intended to take each one of the goals of the elected body, show its connection to the strategic plan, and detail not only the steps that are proposed to be taken in the coming fiscal year, but also describe what resources will be needed to achieve the goals. It's also an opportunity to develop outcome measures that will help indicate effectiveness in realizing goals established by the elected body.*

» *Inputs can help with things like efficiency, but do not necessarily draw our focus to the things that matter to residents and other stakeholders. Outcomes help us focus on results and effectiveness, the things that impact quality of life for our residents. That's what we need to measure.*

» *Our recommendation is that the strategic planning committee have an opportunity to meet quarterly and no less than twice a year to review progress in terms of plan implementation. This is an appropriate time for administration to share outcome measures. Without regularly returning to the elected body and reporting progress, the plan will be soon forgotten and it is likely that your community will lapse into their default mode of doing things the way they've always been done.*

» *As you already know how much time it took you to produce your first plan, leave yourself that amount of time in the planning process prior to the expiration of your current plan. We generally recommend mobilizing the planning process anywhere from a year to a year and three months before the end of the prior planning period.*

9

EATING YOUR VEGETABLES:
HOW TO DEVELOP A CADENCE OF EXECUTION

———

"Without strategy, execution is aimless.
Without execution, strategy is useless."
— Morris Chang, CEO of TSMC

A couple of years ago, I had the following exchange with my then
four-year-old daughter. I pulled a partially filled bag of marshmal-
lows from the pantry to make some Rice Krispies treats for the kids.
When Sofía saw the bag, she ran to the kitchen and announced, "Those
are bad for your body . . . I'll take one."

Most of us know what's good for us and what isn't. We know that
we should eat our vegetables, go to the gym, and avoid too many
sweets. Knowing and doing are two very different things. Someone I
really respect is fond of saying, "What we know is not always reflected
in what we do."

This is especially evident in the realm of strategic planning. While there
are elements of the planning process that can be a lot of work, planning
is the relatively easy part. Execution is hard. Planning is accomplished

175

over a period of weeks or months. Execution takes years of sustained, consistent effort.

We have learned after observing hundreds of organizations' attempts at executing against a strategic plan that the cadence of execution is a critical element in ensuring the realization of the vision laid out by the plan. This cadence ensures that you will look at the plan frequently enough that it will remain top of mind. New Year's resolutions don't generally work. In fact, one study of more than 5,000 individuals and their resolutions found that fewer than 400 actually followed through on those resolutions.[19] We're excited about going to the gym for a couple of weeks in January and then we get lost in the pattern of life that existed before the day we bought a gym membership and made that resolution to exercise.

Organizations are no different. After all, they're made up of people. Without a deliberate plan to change the "pattern of life" that existed prior to the creation of the strategic plan, our organizational New Year's resolutions are just as likely to fall victim to the same inertia that brings down our personal resolutions. The cadence of execution is the center-piece of that deliberate plan.

Before launching into a discussion of how to establish an effective cadence of execution, it's worthwhile to point out something about the community-based strategic planning process itself. If you have followed the recommendations in the previous chapters to establish an advisory committee, go through the process of soliciting citizen feedback, draft a community-based strategic plan based on that feedback, formally adopt that plan, and create goals and a business plan aligned with the strategic plan, you are much more likely to follow through on your New Year's resolution than if you had merely gotten together a few department

---

[19] Joseph Grenny, David Maxfield, and Andrew Shimberg, "How to Have Influence," *MIT Sloan Management Review* 50, no. 1 (2008): 47–52.

heads and elected officials for an offsite and come up with a strategic plan. Why is that?

You have heard us repeat the refrain, the broader the base of participation in the plan's creation, the greater the survivability of the plan. There are powerful social forces at play when you involve an advisory committee and the participation of as many citizens as you can muster. It's harder for elected officials and staff to disregard the "New Year's resolutions" in the plan because of the social pressure that accumulates. The advisory committee, for their part, will be intensely interested in seeing the elements of the plan come to fruition and will be inclined to remind elected officials and staff when they see a lack of execution. The cadence of execution then surrounds these powerful sources of social influence with the structure that will dramatically increase your odds of successful follow-through.

Likewise, powerful motivation comes from connecting the relatively mundane tasks of execution with the inspirational vision for what your community can become. The community-based strategic plan keeps people's sights on the vision and helps them see how the work they do today is connected to that vision. It's one thing to build a capital replacement plan. It's quite another to create that plan in the context of citizen priorities. It transforms a dull spreadsheet into a crusade for quality of life. It's one thing to know that your rates are covering your operating costs as well as capital replacement needs. It's quite another to know that you're building the fiscal sustainability for future generations that your residents have requested. "Here's the chicken sandwich that you ordered. If you'd like something else, let's talk, but if you want a fiscally responsible water fund, here's what it looks like."

Here are a few important elements to consider in developing your cadence:

FREQUENCY

According to research conducted by Deloitte, individuals and organizations that engage in a quarterly process of goal setting and accountability are nearly 4 times more likely to be in the top quartile of performers when compared with those that engage in an annual process.[20] It makes sense that more frequent progress evaluations would lead to improved performance. In this way, when we forget about our New Year's resolutions, we aren't waiting an entire year before realizing that no progress has been made.

There is a point at which the benefits of more frequent monitoring may begin to diminish. Opening the oven every couple of minutes to see if the cake is done yet probably just slows things down. You'll want to give careful consideration to the right frequency for your organization. However, here is a general outline that we have found to work well for most municipal governments.

> » *Monthly Staff Leadership Meetings – This can typically be accomplished in 90 minutes or less and serves as an update on progress relative to key next steps in the business plan. Regularly holding these meetings will also improve the rigor of your business plan. For example, if you have failed to establish clear outcome measures in your business plan, it will become abundantly clear as you pull out the plan and attempt to review progress. Ideally, your business plan will reach a level of detail that clearly articulates who does what, by when, and how you will follow up.*

> » *Quarterly Leadership Offsites – These meetings need not take more than two or three hours and should be focused solely on the strategic initiatives. Don't allow day-to-day matters onto the agenda. Holding them offsite underscores their importance and tends to minimize distractions from day-to-day business. Get your leadership out of the office*

---

[20] The Economist, March 5, 2015, http://www.economist.com/news/business/21645745-management-goal-setting-making-comeback-its-flaws-supposedly-fixed-quantified-serf

*once a quarter to refocus on the most important priorities
and it will pay huge dividends in execution.*

» *Quarterly Updates with the elected body – This is your
opportunity to highlight progress made, potential obstacles, and any areas of concern. It's also another chance
to keep the tenets of your strategic plan in front of the
elected body.*

» *Annual Update from the Strategic Planning Advisory
Committee – Ideally this will take place just prior to or in
conjunction with your annual goal setting retreat. It helps
set the right tone for the goal setting process. This allows
goals to be set in the context of in-process initiatives and
serves as a good reminder of the strategic directives and
initiatives that still need attention and focus.*

» *Annual Goal Setting Retreat – We recommend holding this
session prior to the start of your budgeting process. This
ensures that the goals of the elected body, carefully aligned
with the directives of the strategic plan become the basis
for resource allocation decisions in the budget.*

CLEAR ACCOUNTABILITY

It is beyond the scope of this book to go into a great level of detail
on accountability and follow-up. There are volumes written on the topic.
However, as it relates to the strategic plan and business plan that we recommend you develop, we will add one more element that can improve
accountability and follow-up.

Regarding your business plan, it is critical that you answer four key
questions with respect to each component.

1. *Who?*
2. *Does what?*
3. *By when?*
4. *How will you follow up?*

Let's assume that one of the initiatives for your fiscal sustainability directive is to develop a long-term capital replacement plan for each of your enterprise funds. Let's further assume that the elected body has prioritized this at the goal setting retreat and that it has therefore found its way into your business plan. It is critical that you establish who will ultimately be responsible for creating the capital replacement plans and clearly articulate the expected parameters of that deliverable. Do you just want an excel spreadsheet with a list of items, dates, and amounts? Are you looking for a more formal report with analysis and conclusions? Do you also want to incorporate a rate study to evaluate the revenue implications of a fully-funded capital plan? These sorts of things need to be clearly articulated to ensure effective execution. It may seem obvious, but when do you want to have this done? Often, the answer to this question is not sufficiently clear. Lastly, how will you follow up at the deadline with the individual task owner. It's critical to establish this expectation up front so that nothing comes as a surprise.

If you are serious about execution, we have found it can be especially helpful to develop a detailed 90-day plan that gets rolled forward every month and a 12-month plan with less detail. The purpose of the 90-day look is to ensure that you don't lose sight of what needs to happen next week and next month in order to continue progress on the plan.

There are a number of software tools that have recently become available which enable tracking of specific initiatives and overall directives. These tools can provide full transparency to the elected body and even a measure of transparency to citizens. Whether you use a sophisticated tool or just an Excel spreadsheet, the key is to track progress and follow up regularly.

If you've made it through the community-based strategic planning process, that is only the first step. The ultimate measure of any strategic planning endeavor is the degree to which the plan is executed. To quote Peter Drucker, "Strategy is a commodity. Execution is an art." Your effectiveness as an elected official or municipal administrator will in large part be determined by your ability to develop good systems of execution that align with the priorities laid out in your strategic plan.

TAKEAWAYS

» *Establish a cadence of execution. You don't need to open the proverbial oven every few minutes to see if the cake is done, but should establish periodic checks (more often than annually) to monitor progress.*

» *Leverage the momentum of the strategic planning process itself in building out your business plans. Execution against citizen priorities can be relatively mundane. Be sure to draw people's focus to why that execution is important and how it will make an impact for the community.*

» *Schedule periodic meetings (offsite where possible to create a sense of importance and focus) when you will revisit the progress you have made on specific items in the business plan.*

» *Create clear lines of accountability. It's as simple as asking who, does what, by when, and how will we follow up?*

EPILOGUE
A FINAL WORD: CAVEATS AND ADVICE

——

"All our dreams can come true, if we have the courage to pursue them."
— Walt Disney

I t is a relatively simple thing to write a book about strategic planning. It is a complex thing to assist people in coalescing around a vision. People themselves, and this will be the understatement of the book, are extremely complex. You may certainly follow every morsel of advice provided within these pages, flawlessly implement the techniques described, and yet remain less than successful in realizing the fruits for which you had originally hoped. The harsh reality is that your citizens and civic leaders enjoy a great deal of personal agency. That is why this book describes how to plan your community strategically, not how to make your community into a utopia. Regardless of the best-laid plans, people are going to do what people are going to do.

Some of the challenges that may confront a community at any given time include political change, economic crises, and man-made or natural disasters. Any one of these may require a refocus of resources and attention on issues that weren't originally articulated in your strategic plan. So, the first word of advice we leave with you at the conclusion of this book is to remain light on your feet and flexible. Sometimes the wind simply shifts and you are required to address the issues at hand.

In one of the communities that we assisted, a municipal election was slated in their first strategic planning cycle (the second year of the plan's implementation). That election blew a new political influence into the elected body. A mayor and an at-large council member, who had run jointly on the same platform, narrowly emerged victorious. Instead of collaborating with their incumbent colleagues and seeking consensus on the council, they brought to the elected body a contentious and disruptive environment including taking legal action against one another. Their behavior was so disruptive, that the council was forced to expend precious energy and attention in areas and on issues that drew focus away from the strategic plan. Yet, through it all, the plan remained perhaps the only common frame of reference shared by the incumbents and these newly elected officials, despite the chaos. Just like it did in this community, circumstances for your community may change in the middle of plan implementation and resources may be drawn to address needs originally unrelated to the strategic plan, but the plan itself will provide your community with a rudder that allows it to navigate through troubled waters and emerge in a much better condition than it would have without a plan.

I once "enjoyed" a lunch with a prominent developer in a community I managed. He was the kind of guy who was hyper-energetic and prone to dominate conversations. I concluded that my best strategy was to eat my lunch and allow him to talk. This turned out to be the only strategy. As the lunch progressed, the developer lectured me regarding the litany of government intrusions and general obstacles that municipalities perpetrate against virtuous, freedom-loving developers. Near the conclusion of the lunch, with my meal consumed and his untouched, he began to criticize our city's economic development

vision/strategic plan, saying that it was a complete waste of time and resources and that it was unlikely that anything we had envisioned would actually come to pass. The only thing I recall saying during that lunch appointment was my response to this indictment. I stated, "You may be absolutely correct in that we may not turn out to be anything like the plan describes; but because of the plan, we're going to be a lot better off than we would have been without it."

That's really what strategic planning is all about. It's about lifting your community to a place that it would likely not have arrived without the plan. It's also about re-engaging your citizens in self-governance, building trust, instilling ownership in local government, maximizing the effectiveness of dollars spent, and providing your policymakers with the foundation for making tough decisions. If the plan achieves these, you were successful indeed.

In closing, we leave you with some words of advice regarding the strategic planning process that, if followed, will maximize your chances of a successful experience. Here they are in no particular order of importance:

Do Remain Flexible

We touched on this at the beginning of this chapter. Your strategic plan is a guide. It is not scripture. Speaking of this, there was a story in the New Testament that relates an incident when Jesus was criticized by his detractors for allowing his disciples to engage in an activity on the Sabbath that was specifically prohibited. His response was that the Sabbath was made for man, not man made for the Sabbath.[21] Likewise, the strategic plan is *your* tool. You are *not* a creature of the plan. Don't be so rigid in applying it that it inhibits you from realizing your primary directive. The reality is that things change. This is why we recommend that the strategic planning committee and local leaders regularly review the plan's progress. It is also appropriate to adjust, modify, tweak, or otherwise adapt the plan as time moves forward. When the plan is

---

[21] The Holy Bible, New Testament, Mark 2:27.

modified in the middle of the planning cycle, this should always be ratified publicly and officially.

Do Involve Your Citizens

Regardless of the emphasis we have placed on citizen inclusion, the temptation may persist to limit or even eliminate citizen participation in the creation of your strategic plan. Resist this temptation! We realize that you may be facing an environment in your community where citizens are hostile toward all levels of governance. Such indignation has become almost a part of popular culture. However, unhappy citizens are generally so because they feel disengaged. You are not going to better this situation by excluding them from the strategic planning process. Besides, even if you believe that you could put together a plan for your community in a much more efficient and effective manner without the participation of your citizens, not only may you be exacerbating citizen disengagement, but the chances are that you will end up providing your community with "hamburgers" instead of the "chicken sandwiches" they originally ordered. It should be abundantly clear to those who have read this book that our position is "strategic planning without citizen involvement is not strategic planning at all."

Don't Leave Your Staff Behind

On the other side of the bell curve, we may get so much into the citizen engagement element that we forget about one of our most important publics. Don't forget who is going to have to ultimately implement the plan: your staff. It is therefore critical that you include municipal staff as a stakeholder just as you would any other important group. Their inclusion and feedback are extremely necessary from the very beginning of the planning exercise to the implementation of the plan itself.

Do Obtain the Support of Your Elected Officials

You may not be able to capture enthusiasm for strategic planning from every member of your community or even from all staff, but you had better get the support of your elected body. That doesn't mean that every one of your council or commission members needs to be as terribly enthusiastic as you. However, there ought to exist strong consensus in support of the strategic planning initiative. A four to three vote and/or an antagonistic elected official or two will doom the strategic planning process. It's better to wait for a more politically opportune time. The last thing you need during the strategic planning process is to fight a dedicated foe or group of opponents.

Do Not Hurry the Process

Your community has existed for perhaps decades or even centuries (for some of you in the Northeast and a few other places in the nation) without a community-based strategic plan. There is no need to hurry the process. There is no drop-dead date by which you need the plan completed that is so important that meeting this deadline is worth compromising the plan itself. The most important component of the strategic planning process is the inclusion element. This may require a lot more time in one community than it does in another. The key to strategic planning success and plan legitimacy is tied directly to broadening the base of participation. Likewise, the process of divining community priorities from the citizen feedback cannot be rushed. While we appreciate schedules, don't diminish your plan simply to meet one.

Do Take the Time to Brand Your Strategic Plan Initiative

We are very bullish on the idea of branding your strategic planning endeavor. The reasons are quite simple. There are a lot of programs and initiatives sponsored by myriad jurisdictions, companies, and other organizations. Your citizens need a means of easily identifying your strategic planning initiative. You don't need to spend a lot or hire a Madison Avenue firm to develop a fancy branding campaign. However, the look and theme of your strategic planning endeavor need to communicate what it is, be inviting and enticing, and present the initiative as something *real*. Communities that skip the step associated with the plan branding risk losing their project in the blizzard of other community programs and initiatives.

Do Not Try to Exclude Special Interest Groups

This is an *inclusive* process. Exclusion of any group risks demonstrating the absolute antithesis of strategic planning. Don't worry about this group or that group hijacking your process (unless such fits the description we provided in chapter 3). The objective is to broaden the base of participation to the degree that single issue or agenda folks simply blend into the multicolored tapestry of community feedback. We realize that there are performing arts people, soccer people, dog lovers, hiking people, nature people, bicycle enthusiasts, people with strong political agendas, left-handed bowlers, bad dancers, municipal hobbyists, etc. While we do not want any one group to dominate the process, excluding a group of citizens or stakeholders from participation, without a darn good reason, will absolutely kill the legitimacy of the plan.

Do Make Sure the Plan Is Ratified

Official elected body ratification of the plan places a punctuation mark at the end of the process that is absolutely essential. It not only serves as a means of communicating the elected body's acceptance of the plan, but in real terms brings finality to the strategic planning process. It likewise communicates the legitimacy of the plan to staff, citizens, and other stakeholders of the community. It signals a green light for implementation.

Do Not Forget to Connect the Strategic Plan to the Budget

As we mentioned, the budget document is the supreme policy statement of the elected body for at least a 12-month period. It makes little sense to go through the effort of composing a strategic plan if it is not going to serve as the basis for goal setting and ultimately resource allocation decisions.

Do Report Progress Often and Keep Your Elected Officials

Apprised and Engaged

Your elected body not only nominated and sustained members of the strategic planning committee, commissioning them to assemble a community strategic plan, but it is perfectly natural and appropriate for them to look at this process as *their* initiative. Just as it is absolutely critical to ensure that your elected body supports the strategic planning process, it is equally critical that they continue to support it. One sure way to lose elected official support for any process is to under-communicate. Take regular advantage of public meetings to offer brief reports to the elected body. Between meetings, at least monthly, it would be appropriate to send out a progress report via email. As we mentioned before, your communication with the elected body should be such that very little surprises them at the final presentation of the plan.

Do Consider Some Help

We do not recommend facilitating a strategic planning process without professional guidance, especially the first time around. There are a variety of reasons for this. First and foremost, you have heard the adage that a prophet is rarely respected in his own land. For whatever reason known perhaps to a scant number of psychologists and anthropologists, there is a level of trust and legitimacy extended to people who come from outside of your community to assist in these types of processes. Second, while it is true that a citizen committee does provide a great degree of independence, this quality is magnified with the use of a professional facilitator. All of this is not to say that you cannot conduct your planning yourself. However, at least the first time around, we encourage you to consider hiring a facilitator.

Do Revise the Plan

One of the biggest mistakes that can be made is assuming that your community-based plan will perpetually be there to guide you into the future. Even in a community that in all regards appears to be caught in a time warp, where little has apparently changed in the last century, it is surprising how much the world around you *will* change. Consider this: in 2001, hardly anyone had ever heard of Osama bin Laden and Al Qaeda, and most would have had a hard time pointing to Afghanistan on a map. Most would have concluded that Barak Obama was a Middle Eastern leader. Many thought a tsunami was a cured meat. If you're like me, an iPad was something you temporarily placed on your eye after cataract surgery. On a technology and municipal level, no one had ever heard of the "Cloud," and few were talking about virtualized servers or body cameras for police. Very few had ever heard of Bell, California, or Ferguson, Missouri. We were simply worried about whether our computers would successfully click over to the new millennium without shutting down the entire world.

It is critically important that you not only commit to revising your plan by the end of five years, but make sure that you revisit your plan on a frequent basis, gauge your effectiveness in realizing the directives of the plan, and consider adjustments that may need to be made during those five years.

Do Not Lose Sight of Execution

Success in strategic planning is probably only 5% strategy and 95% execution. Apart from ensuring that your overall direction aligns with the desires of your citizens, the primary benefit derived from a broad-based strategic planning endeavor is the way in which it increases the odds of follow-through and execution. Throughout the process, you should give serious consideration to how you will ensure effective execution of the plan. This is why doing things like formally adopting the plan, building council goals that are supportive of the plan directives, and building a business plan that gets down to the level of specific action steps and outcome measures are so critical. Don't allow yourself to get so lost in the grandeur of the vision that you fail to put one foot in front of the other and do the hard work of climbing the mountain.

Strategic planning will perhaps perpetually rise to the top of the list of disciplines and classes that we wish had been offered to us when we were going through our graduate programs. Actually, the principles that we've covered in this book should be taught in elementary school. The ideas of pre-thinking or imagining, envisioning, and conceptualizing have been the basis of successful outcomes since the beginning of civilization. Some of the greatest achievements in the ancient world showed obvious indications that they were planned strategically. In fact, archaeologists have discovered the existence of entire villages and cities surrounding the construction site of the great pyramids. There cities were constructed complete with bakeries, breweries, streets, and other infrastructure that would support generations of workers. Even the placement of monolithic structures and objects at Stonehenge show a high degree of strategy, forethought, and planning.

Likewise, our communities are intended to outlast this generation and provide an even higher quality of life for those who will inherit them. It is natural for us to desire conditions to be better for our children than they are for us. It is unfortunately natural to live one day at a time and hope that the future takes care of itself. This is the part of our nature that we need to counter. The time you have spent to read this book is hopefully the first step toward planning your community strategically, re-engaging your citizens in self- governance, and ensuring that your community continues to find success.

APPENDICES:
ELECTED BODY GOALS
IMPLEMENTATION PLAN EXAMPLE

———

INTRODUCTION

In January, the elected body identified five goals for the upcoming fiscal year. These goals, together with initiatives and strategies assembled by our senior staff, are being presented for ratification by the elected body.

In this document you will find each goal (in order of prioritization as assigned by the elected body), a brief explanation of the goal which speaks to its importance and community impact, the relevancy of each goal to the Community Strategic Plan, critical outcomes anticipated from the implementation of the goal, and a description of outcome measures. This plan also attempts to determine possible budget impacts associated with the goals. More specific budget information will be found in the budget proposal itself.

Regardless of the presence of some discussion relative to potential costs, elected officials should remember that this is not a budget proposal. The numbers discussed here are preliminary and speculative. It is hoped that each elected official will provide the municipal manager with the feedback necessary to ensure that these goals and associated initiatives reflect as closely as possible the consensus of the elected body.

GOAL NUMBER ONE: PARKS, TRAILS, AND OPEN SPACE

Goal Statement

"Imagine a community that promotes, develops, and maintains a visually appealing community; that builds property values, and increases the quality of life and pride in our community. As a City, we must engage in a community conversation about how to sustainably maintain parks, trails, and open space; and implement a plan and funding solution to accomplish that objective."

Explanation: This goal speaks to the necessity of beginning a public conversation about parks, trails, and open space sustainability and general community aspects. It is the elected body's expectation that this conversation will focus on a funding solution that will bring our community's commitment to these important assets to an appropriate level and that, as a result, we will begin to see and realize a positive impact to community aesthetics, property values, and overall quality of life.

Relevant Strategic Directive(s)

» *"I want to know that the community I leave to my children will be better than the one I found when I came."*

» *"I want to live in a place that looks and feels like home."*

Critical Outcomes

» *Sustainable parks, trails, and open space support.*

» *Parks Department organization and the establishment of a Parks, Trails, and Open Space Fund.*

» *Improved community aesthetics.*

Strategies and Initiatives

» *Complete a community outreach effort focused on the development of an initiative to bring sustainable structure and funding to parks, trails, and open space.*

» *Provide to the elected body all information and feedback necessary for that body to take action, specific to bringing sustainability and improvements to parks, trails, and open space.*

» *Complete the development of a Parks Department organizational structure that will be sufficient and effective. Integral to this effort, develop and implement a plan to staff the new Parks Department and address capital equipment deficiencies.*

» *Create and implement a deployment plan that will enable the new Parks Department to realize its organizational charter. This plan should address such issues as tree replacement, weed abatement, trail maintenance, public space improvements, capital equipment, improvements and replacements, and park maintenance frequency.*

Outcome Measures

» *Acres of park space maintained. This measure is the product of the number of acres in our park space inventory multiplied by the frequency of maintenance.*

» *Urban trees replaced and added.*

» *Number of citizen complaints regarding public property weeds or other aesthetic elements.*

Possible Budget Impact

» *Approximately $1.7–2 million ongoing from year one.*

Goal Steward

Parks Director

GOAL NUMBER TWO: ECONOMIC DEVELOPMENT

Goal Statement

"Imagine a community that promotes and encourages balance and diversification of the economy through the recruitment of an economic development director with specific skills and knowledge in commercial and industrial development and economic growth, with a proven record and history of success in these fields. Additionally, we need to review and revise the economic development strategic plan with defined measurements and outcomes aligned with the Community Strategic Plan and the vision of the elected body."

Explanation: This goal speaks to the necessity of elevating the attention and energy devoted to economic development. The goal specifically calls for, as a means of accomplishing this, the recruitment of an economic development director. The intention of this recruitment would be to recruit an individual with a track record of business recruitment experience and success. The goal also calls for an examination and subsequent modifications of and to the economic development strategic plan to ensure that it is aligned with the primary directives of the community strategic plan and the vision of the elected body.

Relevant Strategic Directive(s)

» *"I want to live in a place where commercial establishments are modern, convenient, and always improving; and where good jobs are plentiful."*

Critical Outcomes

» *Recruitment of an experienced and successful economic development director, as well as singular attention and energy focused on business recruitment and retention.*

» *Establishment of sufficient funding to support the activities of the economic development director.*

» *Re-examination of the economic development plan, as well as modifications to that plan as necessary.*

» *Greater success in recruiting and retaining businesses.*

Strategies and Initiatives

» *Recruit an experienced and successful economic development director.*

» *Review the economic development strategic plan and modify as needed to align the objectives of this plan with the greater community vision.*

» *Proactively engage the business community and regional partners in order to increase business location and expansion.*

» *Continue to implement the community branding initiative.*

Outcome Measures

» *Business locations and expansions.*

» *Total jobs or employment.*

» *Total retail sales.*

» *Added property value.*

Possible Budget Impact

» *Approximately $200,000 annually beginning in year one.*

Goal Steward

Economic Development Director

GOAL NUMBER THREE: LAND USE

Goal Statement

"Imagine a community where we engage stakeholders to lower densities and improve our design and construction standards for both residential and commercial projects; and encourage use of performance-based planning to achieve higher quality developments."

Explanation: This goal speaks to the necessity of ensuring that the development of remaining space maximizes value and contributions to quality of life. This goal also signals the general need to revisit such fundamental aspects of our planning as densities, performance incentives, and construction standards.

Relevant Strategic Directive(s)

» *"I want to live in a place where our leaders develop and maintain infrastructure that supports growth and stability well into the future."*

» *"I want to live in a place that looks and feels like home."*

Critical Outcomes

» *Higher value and less dense development.*

» *Higher quality and value of commercial construction.*

» *Clearly defined development code and standards that consider future development and encourage higher property values.*

» *Attraction of a higher quality development and contributing residents.*

» *Enhanced community brand.*

Strategies and Initiatives

» *Review and revision of building code to encourage creative pathways that include larger homes and elevated construction standards. Utilize relationships with stakeholders to develop and propose these modifications.*

» *Support for view code enforcement to ensure that new developments do not deteriorate.*

» *Review and propose modifications to current code to ensure new developments remain functional and aesthetically contribute to our community.*

» *Implement an educational program for outreach to*

stakeholders and developers that effectively communi-
cates adopted changes, elevated standards, and commu-
nity expectations.

Outcome Measures
- » *Assessed values.*
- » *New development value.*
- » *Density of new residential development.*

Possible Budget Impact
- » *Undetermined.*

Goal Steward
Planning Director

GOAL NUMBER FOUR: FLEET
Goal Statement
"Imagine a community where we achieve fleet cost reductions through asset management system implementation; determine the best funding mechanisms for vehicle and equipment acquisition; determine and iden-tify a cost/benefit process to replace aging and more expensive fleet units with cost-effective and reliable equipment and vehicles; examine and recommend benefits of acquiring high performing equipment over less reliable and less costly models; and evaluate equipment for use in capacity functions that provide the greatest versatility and adaptability."

Explanation: This goal speaks to the necessity of ensuring that we maximize the value of every fleet dollar in order to en-hance the abilities of our staff to accomplish assigned tasks and provide a high level of service. In so doing, the goal states that we need to consider not only how we acquire fleet units, but also focus on the type, ap-propriateness, and versatility of each new unit.

Relevant Strategic Directive(s)

» *"I want to live in a place where our leaders develop and maintain infrastructure that supports growth and stability well into the future."*

Critical Outcomes

» *Higher functioning fleet.*

» *Enhanced fleet acquisition capabilities.*

» *Fleet units that project an appropriate image and promote a positive brand.*

» *Long-term fleet sustainability.*

Strategies and Initiatives

» *Analyze fleet funding/acquisition methodologies, with specific implementation of a program/policy that maximizes effectiveness of every fleet purchase.*

» *Enhance Fleet Board functionality and effectiveness by increasing coordination and evaluation, as well as speeding fleet unit acquisition.*

» *Develop and propose to the elected body a plan for constructing a new fleet facility.*

Outcome Measures

» *Fleet unit age by class and use.*

» *Fleet downtime.*

» *Total fleet operations and maintenance costs.*

» *Timeliness of fleet acquisitions.*

Possible Budget Impact

» *Although undetermined, it is anticipated that these initiatives will result in lower per unit costs.*

Goal Steward

Public Works Director

GOAL NUMBER FIVE: POLICE

Goal Statement

"Imagine a community where we develop and implement a plan to bring active police staffing to authorized levels, and where we develop a framework and implementation plan to reach appropriate staffing levels."

Explanation: This goal speaks to the necessity of shortening the time frame during which we fill vacant police positions. Not only this, the goal articulates the necessity of not only reaching authorized staffing levels, but also evaluating the effectiveness of that staffing, thus enabling staff to make specific recommendations to the elected body with regard to future staffing and associated funding. In so doing, we also remain cognizant of the necessity of structuring compensation in a way that attracts experienced peace officers, as well as new recruits.

Relevant Strategic Directive(s)

» *"I want to live in a place where my family feels safe."*

Critical Outcomes

» *Shorter time frames from recruitment to on-the-street deployment.*

» *Increased discretionary/patrol time per officer.*

» *Greater capacity to recruit experienced officers.*

Strategies and Initiatives

» *Review and revise as needed police recruitment policies, practices, and compensatory structure in order to enhance our position as an employer of choice.*

» *Compose and present to the elected body, following evaluation of the effects of full deployment on critical outcomes, a timeline, and funding plan associated with adding new officers.*

» *Identify and begin executing a strategy/methodology to*

enhance recruitment efforts of experienced officers from other agencies.

» *Maintain open lines of communication and information between policymakers and the Police Department.*

» *Retain civilian position specifically dedicated to background investigations of candidates.*

Outcome Measures

» *Per officer discretionary time.*

» *Recruitment to on-street time.*

» *Caseload per officer.*

» *Average law enforcement years per officer.*

» *Crime rates. (various)*

Possible Budget Impacts

» *Approximately $50,000 annually to support civilian position.*

» *Adjustments to compensatory structure dependent on analysis findings.*

Goal Steward

Police Chief

ABOUT THE AUTHORS

Rick Davis is a 20-year veteran of city management and an International City and County Management Association (ICMA) Credentialed Manager.

Formerly a corporate public relations director, Rick made his way into the public sector in 1994 via the Office of the Arizona Auditor General. In addition to serving as a city manager for municipalities in Utah, Arizona, and Texas, Rick has assisted local governments from Kabul, Afghanistan, to Sitka, Alaska, and from Dartmouth, Massachusetts, to Daytona Beach, Florida, to identify inefficiencies and plan strategically.

A frequent presenter at conferences and universities, Rick holds a master's degree in public administration and a bachelor's degree in communications, both from Brigham Young University. He is also the author of "Marketing Your Community for Economic Development," an ICMA publication. Rick and his wife Aimee have three children and reside in the Houston Area. *(www.linkedin.com/in/rickdavisma-cm/)*

Dan Griffiths is a strategy and leadership consultant who has worked with hundreds of organizations in the development of their strategic plans, including a number of municipal governments. He facilitates over 75 planning retreats each year.

Dan began his career as an auditor and CPA and then as the CFO at a small private equity firm. He has been consulting in the area of strategic planning for over a decade.

Dan is very active in government and previously served as a member of the Utah State Board of Education. He currently serves on a legislative commission focused on fiscal sustainability and as a senior advisor to the Kem C. Gardner Policy Institute at the University of Utah. Dan is a member of the American Institute of Certified Public Accountants (AICPA) board of directors and together with his wife, Bibiana, is the proud parent of four children. They currently reside in the Salt Lake City area. *(www.linkedin.com/in/dangriffithscpa/)*

For more information, tools, and sample plans, please visit:
www.tannerco.com/municipal-planning

For questions, send an e-mail to *info@tannerco.com*
or contact us at *+1.801.532.7444*